Weiss Ratings' Consumer Guide to Automobile Insurance

Weiss Ratings' Consumer Guide to Automobile Insurance

Spring 2023

GREY HOUSE PUBLISHING

Weiss Ratings
11780 US Highway 1, Suite 201
Palm Beach Gardens, FL 33408
561-627-3300

Published by Grey House Publishing, Inc., located at 4919 Route 22, Amenia, NY 12501; telephone 518-789-8700. Grey House Publishing neither guarantees the accuracy of the data contained herein nor assumes any responsibility for errors, omissions or discrepancies. Grey House Publishing accepts no payment for listing; inclusion in the publication of any organization, agency, institution, publication, service or individual does not imply endorsement of the publisher.

4919 Route 22
PO Box 56
Amenia, NY 12501-0056

Spring 2023 Edition

ISBN: 978-1-63700-603-0
ISSN: 2165-3976

CONTENTS

Terms and Conditions

Weiss Ratings' Mission Statement

Weiss Ratings' mission is to empower consumers, professionals, and institutions with high quality advisory information for selecting or monitoring a financial services company or financial investment. In doing so, Weiss Ratings will adhere to the highest ethical standards by maintaining our independent, unbiased outlook and approach to advising our customers.

About This Guide

Unless your city has a good public transportation system, owning a car is probably essential to your ability to work, play, and generally enjoy a modern lifestyle. And along with car ownership comes the need to purchase automobile insurance. In fact, very few people factor the cost of auto insurance into their decision about which car to buy. What most people don't realize, however, is that it is often very easy to save hundreds of dollars per year on auto insurance by simply educating yourself and shopping around.

This is where Weiss Ratings can help. This publication is designed to give you a good overview of your auto insurance options. It walks you through the considerations for selecting the appropriate type of insurance and coverage levels, plus it gives you instruction on how to find the best price from a strong, reputable insurer.

Best of all, you can rest assured that the information presented here is completely independent and free of bias. Weiss Ratings does not sell insurance, we are not connected with any insurance companies, and we won't make a single penny should you decide to purchase a policy from one of the companies listed in this guide. Our goal is to simply help you make the best decision possible – for you.

Anatomy of an Auto Insurance Policy

At its core, auto insurance is simply a contract between you and your insurance company to protect against financial loss in the unfortunate event that you have an accident. Depending on what you purchase, the insurance coverage can provide financial assistance to:

- repair your vehicle or replace it in the event it is damaged or stolen

- reimburse others if you cause an accident that hurts them or their vehicle

- pay for any medical expenses arising from injuries you or your passengers sustain in an accident

At a minimum, most states require you to have liability insurance coverage to protect others in case you are at fault in an accident. There are two primary kinds of liability coverage that you need:

- **Bodily Injury Liability** is coverage for injuries you might cause to someone else. Most states stipulate a minimum amount of this coverage although you can elect to purchase higher policy limits if you're willing to pay higher premiums. Table 1 shows your state's minimum required policy limits. Note that the coverage amount for bodily injury liability is always stated using two numbers, e.g. $100,000/$300,000. The first number is the maximum amount the policy will pay for damages to one person, and the second number is the maximum amount payable for injuries for the entire accident.

- **Property Damage Liability** is coverage for damage you might cause to someone else's property. Typically this will be damage done to another person's car, but it also covers any other object you hit including buildings, fences, or street signs. Again, most states stipulate a minimum amount of this coverage per accident (see Table 1), with more coverage available at higher premiums. This number is the third one listed, immediately following the two numbers for bodily injury liability protection.

Although optional for drivers in most states, some states may require other types of coverage:

- **Medical Payments or Personal Injury Protection (PIP)** is coverage to treat injuries to you and your passengers, regardless of who is at fault in the accident. This type of coverage may also pay funeral expenses and lost wages in some circumstances. In the event that you have an accident that requires medical payments and you have this coverage, you will be required to pay a certain amount of the cost out of your own pocket, known as the deductible, and the insurance company will pay the remainder of the claim. The higher your deductible, the lower your premiums will be.

- **Under-Insured and Uninsured Motorist Coverage** is protection for you, your passengers, and your vehicle in case you have an accident with an uninsured driver, a hit-and-run driver, or a driver with insufficient insurance coverage. This type of insurance also covers you and your family members as pedestrians if you are injured by a hit-and-run driver.

Finally, there are two additional types of auto insurance to cover the cost of repairs to your car. These coverages are never required by the state, but if you have a loan or lease on your car, your lender will usually require both:

- **Collision** insurance pays to repair damage to your car from a collision, regardless of who is at fault. (In the event that you are not at fault, your insurer will generally try to get the other party's insurance company to reimburse them for the damage to your vehicle.) Collision coverage usually has a deductible between $250 and $1,000 that you must pay toward the repairs before your insurer will pay its portion. As with PIP, the higher your deductible, the lower your premiums will be.

- **Comprehensive** insurance covers your car for everything that is not covered by collision insurance. This includes the cost to replace or repair your vehicle due to theft or damage from things like hail, water, flood, fire, wind, explosion, earthquake, animals, or vandalism. This coverage also has a deductible, which is usually equal to or lower than the deductible on your collision insurance.

Additional Types of Coverage Available to You

In addition to these basic components, insurance companies also offer other add-on coverage's to enhance their customers' policies. These often include:

- **Roadside Assistance** pays for towing charges up to a certain limit. It also includes labor costs for breakdowns that can be repaired on site. If you own an older car that is more prone to breakdown, this type of insurance may be attractive. However, this coverage is not necessary if you already have an auto club membership.

- **Rental Car Reimbursement** pays for the cost of a rental car while your car is being repaired after an accident. The coverage is usually limited to $30 per day, but can vary by insurer. Keep in mind that this type of insurance will not pay for a rental car when yours is in for regular maintenance or repairs unrelated to an accident. It is strictly an add-on to your collision or comprehensive coverage to help you get your car back in working order.

Depending upon your family's vehicle situation, this may or may not be necessary.

- **Gap Insurance for Leased or Financed Vehicles** covers the difference between what the insurance company will pay and the amount you owe on a leased or financed vehicle in the event it is damaged beyond repair. Not all companies offer this coverage. However, some auto leases actually include it as a part of your lease agreement, so be sure to check your lease documents first before purchasing this add-on coverage.

Coverage Required in Your State

Every state has a financial responsibility law requiring its residents to show proof of their ability to pay for any claims arising from an accident, up to a certain amount. As you might expect, most people purchase auto insurance simply to comply with these laws, sticking with the bare minimum coverage limits mandated by their state. Table 1 provides a list of the current liability policy limits required by each state.

Note that the liability limits are shown in a series of three numbers. The first number refers to the maximum amount the insurer will pay for one individual's bodily injury. The second number refers to the maximum amount the insurer will pay for all people injured in an accident. And the third number refers to the maximum amount of property damage the insurer will pay for. For example, Alabama's limits of 25/50/25 mean that Alabama requires its residents to purchase at least $25,000 of bodily injury coverage for one person, at least $50,000 of bodily injury coverage for all parties injured in a single accident, and at least $25,000 of property damage coverage. These figures represent the minimum amount of coverage you must purchase, but they are also the maximum amount your insurer will have to pay in the event of an accident. So, what happens if you purchase the bare minimum required but cause an accident where the costs exceed these limits?

In that case, the other party may sue you to collect what your insurance company did not pay. If you don't have many assets, this may not be a concern for you. Otherwise, you may find it worthwhile to purchase higher policy limits than the minimums required by your state. In fact, most insurers and consumer groups recommend drivers hold minimum liability coverage of $100,000 per person and $300,000 per accident for bodily injury. This is usually combined with a $100,000 limit for property damage given the high cost of many cars these days, plus the potential for damaging other types of property at the accident scene.

Table 1. Automobile Financial Responsibility Limits and Enforcement By State

State	Insurance Required	Liability Limits (1)	State	Insurance Required	Liability Limits (1)
Alabama	BI & PD Liab	25/50/25	Nebraska	BI & PD Liab, UM, UIM	25/50/25
Alaska	BI & PD Liab	50/100/25	Nevada	BI & PD Liab	25/50/20
Arizona	BI & PD Liab	25/50/15	New Hampshire	FR only	25/50/25
Arkansas	BI & PD Liab, PIP	25/50/25	New Jersey	BI & PD Liab, PIP, UM, UIM	15/30/5 (5)
California	BI & PD Liab	15/30/5 (2)	New Mexico	BI & PD Liab	25/50/10
Colorado	BI & PD Liab	25/50/15	New York	BI & PD Liab, PIP, UM, UIM	25/50/10 (6)
Connecticut	BI & PD Liab, UM, UIM	25/50/25	North Carolina	BI & PD Liab, UM, UIM	30/60/25
Delaware	BI & PD Liab, PIP	25/50/10 (3)	North Dakota	BI & PD Liab, PIP, UM, UIM	25/50/25
Florida	PD Liab, PIP	10/20/10 (3)	Ohio	BI & PD Liab	25/50/25
Georgia	BI & PD Liab	25/50/25	Oklahoma	BI & PD Liab	25/50/25(3)
Hawaii	BI & PD Liab, PIP	20/40/10	Oregon	BI & PD Liab, PIP, UM, UIM	25/50/20
Idaho	BI & PD Liab	25/50/15	Pennsylvania	BI & PD Liab, PIP	15/30/5
Illinois	BI & PD Liab, UM, UIM	25/50/20	Rhode Island	BI & PD Liab	25/50/25
Indiana	BI & PD Liab	25/50/25	South Carolina	BI & PD Liab, UM	25/50/25
Iowa	BI & PD Liab	20/40/15	South Dakota	BI & PD Liab, UM, UIM	25/50/25
Kansas	BI & PD Liab, PIP	25/50/25	Tennessee	BI & PD Liab	25/50/15 (3)
Kentucky	BI & PD Liab, PIP	25/50/25 (3)	Texas	BI & PD Liab, PIP	30/60/25
Louisiana	BI & PD Liab	15/30/25	Utah	BI & PD Liab, PIP	25/65/15 (3)
Maine	BI & PD Liab, UM	50/100/25(3), (4)	Vermont	BI & PD Liab, PIP, UM, UIM	25/50/10
Maryland	BI & PD Liab, PIP, UM, UIM	30/60/15(3)	Virginia	BI & PD Liab (7), UM, UIM	30/60/20
Massachusetts	BI & PD Liab, PIP	20/40/5	Washington	BI & PD Liab	25/50/10
Michigan	BI & PD Liab, PIP	20/40/10	Wash. D.C.	BI & PD Liab, UM	25/50/10
Minnesota	BI & PD Liab, PIP, UM, UIM	30/60/10	West Virginia	BI & PD Liab, UM	25/50/25
Mississippi	BI & PD Liab	25/50/25	Wisconsin	BI & PD Liab, UM, Medpay	25/50/10
Missouri	BI & PD Liab, UM	25/50/25	Wyoming	BI & PD Liab	25/50/20
Montana	BI & PD Liab	25/50/20			

1. Compulsory Coverage:

   BI Liab = Bodily injury liability

   PD Liab = Property damage liability

   UM = Uninsured motorist

   PD = Physical damage

   Med = First party (policyholder) medical expenses

   UIM = Underinsured Motorist

   PIP = Personal Injury Protection. Mandatory in no-fault states. Includes medical, rehabilitation, loss of earnings and funeral expenses. In some states PIP includes essential services such as child care

   FR = Financial responsibility only. Insurance not compulsory

1. **The first two numbers refer to bodily injury (BI) liability limits and the third number to property damage (PD) liability. For example, 20/40/10 means coverage up to $40,000 for all persons injured in an accident, subject to a limit of $20,000 for one individual, and $10,000 coverage for property damage.**

2. **Low-cost policy limits for low-income drivers in the California Automobile Assigned Risk Plan are 10/20/3.**

3. **Instead of policy limits, policyholders can satisfy the requirement with a combined single limit policy. Amounts vary by state.**

4. **In addition, policyholders must carry coverage for medical payments.**

5. **Basic policy (optional) limits are 10/10/5. Uninsured and underinsured motorist coverage not available under the basic policy but uninsured and underinsured motorist coverage is required under the standard policy. Special Automobile Insurance Policy available for certain drivers which only covers emergency treatment and a $10,000 death benefit.**

6. **In addition, policyholders must have 50/100 for wrongful death coverage.**

7. **Compulsory to buy insurance or pay an uninsured motorists vehicle (UMV) fee to the state department of motor vehicles.**

*On January 1, 2025 limits will be increased to 50/100/25.

Note: State laws regarding mandatory requirements for uninsured and underinsured motorists vary. State departments of insurance should be consulted to determine whether these coverages are compulsory.

Source: American Property Casualty Insurers Association; state departments of insurance. (www.iii.org).

"No-Fault" Insurance

Aside from specifying required liability limits, some states also have what is known as a "no-fault" liability law. In such states, each person in an accident is covered by their own insurance company, regardless of who caused the accident. Although you may feel such a system is unfair if you are not the one who caused the accident, you will undoubtedly appreciate the ease with which you can file a claim since you're only dealing with your own insurance company. Plus, this system helps to lower insurance costs and keep policy costs down by eliminating most small court claims and limiting lawsuits to only those involving serious injuries.

Twelve states currently require all auto policies to be no-fault policies:

- Florida
- Hawaii
- Kansas
- Kentucky
- Massachusetts
- Michigan
- Minnesota
- New Jersey
- New York
- North Dakota
- Pennsylvania
- Utah

In these states, if you choose no-fault insurance, you are immune from being sued and from suing other drivers for non-economic damages like pain and suffering. However, if you choose traditional liability coverage, you can sue and be sued if the other driver also has traditional coverage. Because the "no-fault" choice provides immunity from being sued, it tends to be the choice of bad drivers. Even so, these same limits on lawsuits also tend to make no-fault coverage the cheaper option. Consequently, this system is often charged with unfairly punishing good drivers.

Eleven states allow you to add a no-fault provision to your auto insurance policy in order to facilitate claims, but do not restrict your ability to sue the other party in an accident.

These states, known as "Add-On" states, are:

- Arkansas
- Delaware
- D.C.
- Maryland
- New Hampshire
- Oregon

- South Dakota
- Texas
- Virginia
- Washington
- Wisconsin

In addition, drivers in the District of Columbia can choose no-fault or a traditional liability policy, but if they choose no-fault, they have 60 days after an accident to decide if they want the no-fault benefits or wish to pursue a claim against the other person in the accident.

The remaining 27 states have regular liability policies with no specific limitations on your ability to sue for damages.

Things Your Policy Won't Cover

In addition to stating the types of injury or damage that are covered, your auto insurance policy will also have a list of things that are not covered, called "exclusions." The most common exclusions are:

- **Intentional injury** – Your policy will not pay for damages if you intentionally hit another vehicle or piece of property.

- **Property owned or transported** – This refers to personal items carried in your vehicle. For example, if you are carrying golf clubs in your car and they are damaged during an accident, your auto policy will not pay to repair or replace them. However, your homeowners policy may provide such coverage.

- **Public or livery conveyance** – If you use your car to transport people or property for a fee (e.g. as a taxi), your car will not be covered under your personal auto policy. Instead, you would need to purchase a separate commercial auto policy. This exclusion doesn't apply to car pools.

- **Other business uses** – Even if you run a business that doesn't involve transporting people or property, your car will not be covered under your personal auto policy when it is being used for business purposes. You would instead need to purchase a separate commercial auto policy.

- **Motorized vehicles with fewer than four wheels** – Motorcycles, mopeds, scooters, all-terrain vehicles, snowmobiles, and other similar-type vehicles are not automatically covered under your auto policy. However, coverage for these vehicles may generally be added onto your policy for an additional fee (see below).

Insuring Your Other Vehicles

Auto insurance policies are designed to only cover your personal car or truck. Nevertheless, you can usually add other coverage's to an auto policy for other forms of transportation such as a motorcycle, all-terrain vehicle, recreational vehicle (RV), snowmobile, jet ski, or boat. Adding coverage for any of these vehicles is known as attaching a "rider" onto your auto policy.

Collector and antique cars also require special coverage, but this is usually a bit harder to get. Many companies won't insure vehicles more than 20 years old, except possibly on a rider with restricted usage. That's not to say that you won't be able to find coverage. In fact, some insurers specialize in high value collector and antique vehicles that are used infrequently. You just won't be able to add such coverage onto the policy covering your everyday vehicle. If you own a collector or antique automobile, contact your local car club and they should be able to recommend an agent to assist you with this coverage.

Exotic, high-performance, and high-value vehicle owners may also have trouble finding coverage. For example, there are not a lot of insurance companies that want to take on the risk of a Ferrari, Rolls Royce, or Bentley since the cost to repair or replace them is so high. If you own a car of this type, you'll want to contact an insurance agent (or possibly your auto dealer) and let him assist you in finding insurance coverage.

How Premiums are Determined

Insurance companies take a wide range of factors into consideration when determining how much you will have to pay in premiums. These include:

- **Amount of coverage purchased** – The higher the policy's maximum coverage limits, the higher your premium will be. You may be able to get away with the minimums required by your state, but go ahead and ask for pricing on higher limits before making that decision. Depending on the other factors listed below, you may be able to substantially increase your protection for a very modest increase in your premiums.

- **Amount of deductible** – The deductible is the portion of the claim you must pay before the insurance company will pay the remainder. Deductibles typically range from $250 to $1,000. As you might expect, the higher the deductible, the lower your premium will be. (This applies to collision, comprehensive, and personal injury protection.)

- **Type of Car** – Next to the amount of coverage you purchase, the type of car you drive is the second most important factor in determining your premium. Due to the nature of their drivers, owning a sports car will usually drive up your insurance premium. Likewise, sport utility vehicles (SUVs) are usually more expensive to insure while family sedans are usually less expensive to insure. This varies somewhat by insurer based on each insurer's own assessment of the cost to repair the vehicle, its safety features, and its propensity for being stolen.

- **Driving history** – The insurance company uses your driving record as an indication of the type of driver you are for determining how much risk they are accepting. Therefore, if you have a history of auto insurance claims or traffic violations, your insurer will consider you a higher risk driver and will raise your premium rate accordingly.
  Drivers with very poor records or a DUI conviction can even have difficulty finding an insurer who will cover them at all. If you fall into this category, you may have to turn to your state's Assigned Risk Plan – there's one in every state – which assigns you to an insurer. The state will require that insurer to provide you with coverage but will also allow them to charge you significantly higher rates.

- **Gender** – Statistically speaking, men have more accidents than women. As such, men tend to be charged higher premiums.

- **Age** – Statistics again indicate that younger and older drivers tend to be the riskiest. In 2019 drivers age 16 to 20 years old accounted for 5.2 percent of all the drivers involved in fatal crashes and 22.3 percent of all the drivers involved in all police-reported crashes.[1] If you are a young driver, expect to pay higher premiums. This becomes less of a factor at age 21 and is removed as a factor at age 25, after which you'll enjoy many years before you grow old enough for your insurer to consider you high risk once again. Premiums begin to creep up again for older drivers, as statistics support their riskier status. According to the National Highway Traffic Safety Administration, 15.2 percent of all people killed on the road in 2019 were 65 or older.

- **Marital status** – Married people tend to have fewer accidents than single people, so you will likely see a discount in your premium if you are married.

- **Other drivers in your household** – When determining your premium, your insurer will not only look at all of the above factors for you, it will also take these factors into consideration for everyone in your household (any other licensed drivers in your house must be disclosed on your application). That means a teenage son would bring your premium way up, but a spouse with a clean driving record would help bring the premium down.

- **Location** – Insurers must get their premium rates approved in each state where they are licensed, leading to a variation in rates between states based on the insurer's claims history in the state. For example, drivers in Florida have more accidents than drivers in Wyoming, so Florida drivers pay higher premium rates – even for the same insurer insuring the same driver and vehicle. And within Florida, there are some areas that have more accidents than others (e.g., highly urban areas like Miami) which lead to even higher rates for drivers located within those areas.

---

[1] Insurance Information Institute (www.iii.org)

- **Vehicle usage** – The more you drive, the more opportunity there is for you to be in an accident. Therefore, you'll find the premiums lower for your "weekend car" than for a car you use to drive 30 miles each way to work. The more you drive the vehicle, the higher the premiums will be.

- **Credit Scores** – Insurance companies have recently started using credit scores as a predictor of future claims activity. There has been much debate about the validity of this factor, but research, including a 2003 study by EPIC Actuaries, that show a correlation between credit scores and claims activity. The law does not allow an insurer to use your credit history as the sole factor in determining your premiums. Your credit score can, however, be used against you to decline coverage or as one of several factors used to set your premium. Not all companies use credit scores, so if your credit history is particularly bad, it is all the more important that you shop around for an auto policy from an insurer that does not use credit scores as a factor in setting its premiums. This could easily save you hundreds of dollars per year.

Although these are the basic factors that every insurance company uses in setting its premiums, the amount you pay will still vary from company to company based upon each insurer's underwriting model (the process of assessing your risk and pricing your policy accordingly). Some insurance companies weight some factors more heavily than others. In addition, one company may have had a high level of claims in a particular state, forcing it to raise premiums in that state, whereas another company in the same state may have had a low level of claims there, allowing them to lower premiums in that state.

Also, some insurers charge a flat fee for your liability coverage, regardless of the vehicle you drive, while others base your premium for liability coverage on the type of vehicle.

Ways to Save Money on Your Premium

The most effective way to save money on your auto insurance premium is to be a safe driver. The fewer accidents and traffic violations you have, the more insurers you'll have bidding for your business and the lower their rate quotes will be. Other ways to lower your premium are to:

- **Take a driver safety course.** If you've been ticketed for an accident or some other violation, the state will remove it from your driving record when you take a driver safety course. The required courses vary from state to state and can help to keep your driving record as clean as possible. In addition, almost all insurance companies will lower your premium just for taking it. So, even if you haven't been ticketed, you can still take a driver safety course to save money.

- **Increase your deductible.** Ask your insurer for premium quotes using different deductible levels to see how much you could save by covering a greater portion of an accident cost out of your own pocket. It may be worth it to go with a higher deductible, particularly if you're a safe driver who is less likely to be in an accident or if you've got the financial capacity to pay a higher deductible in the event of an accident.

- **Forego comprehensive and/or collision coverage.** If the value of your vehicle is not that high, you might want to consider going without comprehensive and/or collision coverage. For instance, if your car is more than ten years old or if it already has significant body damage, the cost of these coverages over a year or two could exceed the value of the vehicle entirely.

- **Compare prices regularly.** Shop your policy around by getting premium quotes from other insurers every year or two. You don't necessarily have to change companies, but this is generally a worthwhile exercise. It's relatively easy to do and you could find another insurer that will save you a significant amount of money on your auto insurance.

- **Use the same company for homeowners and auto insurance.** Almost all insurers will give you a discount on your premium if you purchase insurance for both your home and your car from them. But, even with this discount, you could end up paying more than you would by shopping for the least expensive coverage from two separate, unrelated insurers.

- **Take advantage of group discounts.** If you are a member of a national group like AAA, AARP, AMA, ABA, etc. ask your agent if there are any special discounts for your group. And if you or your parents were in the military, be sure to get a rate quote from USAA, a company that specifically caters to military personnel. As with other discounts, you'll want to make sure that the discounted policy is indeed less expensive than your other alternatives. In other words, don't buy it just because the insurer is giving a discount to your group.

- **Choose a vehicle that is less expensive to insure.** When you're in the process of buying a new car, that is the perfect time to factor insurance costs into your selection decision. Ask your insurer (as well as other insurers) for premium quotes on a couple of different vehicles that you are considering so you can see if one would cost you more from an insurance standpoint. Premiums are generally lower for small sedans, minivans, and mid-sized family sedans than they are for sports cars and large SUVs. Also, make sure your prospective purchase isn't high on the stolen vehicle list since insurers use this list heavily in setting their premium rates. See Table 3 for the most and least expensive vehicles to insure.

- **Choose a hybrid vehicle.** Some insurers offer discounted insurance rates to hybrid drivers in some states. Research shows that hybrid drivers pose a lower insurance risk because they drive fewer miles and have better driving pattern and record. Make sure to inquire about how choosing a hybrid might save you money.

- **Explore Usage Based Insurance (UBI) options.** Insurers are increasingly using new technology to determine how safely the car is being driven and to gather data on driving habits. Insurance companies offer programs that focus solely on miles driven or tracks driving behavior as well as miles driven. Your miles driven, time of day and hard braking data is tracked by installing an electronic device in your car and may result in lower insurance rates for safe driving. Ask about these voluntary programs when you shop for auto insurance.

Table 3. 10 Most and Least Expensive 2023 Vehicles to Insure [2]

Most Expensive	Least Expensive
1. Quattroporte	1. Forester 2.5I Wilderness
2. Quattroporte Modena Q4	2. Venue SE
3. M8 Competiton Gran coupe	3. CR-V LX
4. Panamera Turbo S E-Hybrid Ex	4. CX-30 S
5. RS E-tron GT	5. C-HR XLE
6. Panamera Turbo	6. C-HR NightShade
7. Model S Plaid	7. CX-30 S Premium
8. M8 Competition XDrive	8. CR-V EX
9. Taycan Turbo S	9. Seltos LX
10. R8 5.2L V10 Quattro Performance	10. HR-V EX

- **Use your clean credit report to your advantage.** Depending upon the laws in your state, insurance companies can use your credit history to grant or deny coverage or as a factor in setting your premium rate. So be sure to get a copy of your credit report and make sure any erroneous information is removed (this is a good idea even when you're not shopping for auto insurance). You'll usually be given the option of whether or not to grant the insurance company access to your credit report. So, if you have decent credit, let them see it and it could save you some money.

- **Ask about discounts specifically for young drivers.** If you have a young driver in your house, be sure to ask if your insurer gives any discounts for taking a drivers' education course or getting good grades. Such discounts are becoming more popular these days and companies attempt to better assess their risk of an accident.

---

[2] Source: Insure.com.

- **Pay your premium in advance.** If you can afford it, pay your full annual or semi annual policy premium up front. Some companies actually give you a discount for doing so, while others will charge an extra fee ($3 to $5 each month) if you elect to pay your premiums monthly.

With the growth of the Internet, there is a wealth of additional free information available to help you save money or get better coverage on your auto insurance. See the Appendix for a listing of useful websites.

How to Shop for an Auto Policy

Now that you realize the value of shopping around to get the best rate on your auto insurance policy, the next step is to take action. There are three possible routes to go – agents, direct writers, and the Internet – and you should feel free to pursue any or all of them depending on the amount of time and effort you're willing to devote.

Agents

Most people prefer face-to-face interaction and therefore opt to work with an insurance agent. There are pros and cons to this approach, however. On the positive side, a knowledgeable agent can walk you through the entire purchasing process, answering any questions you may have and helping you to select the policy components that are right for you. An agent can also be particularly helpful when you have a claim by assisting you in your dealings with the claims adjuster and the insurance company.

On the downside, not all insurance agents are created equal. Some have lousy customer service, essentially negating the benefits listed above. And others are so focused on increasing their commissions that they try to push you into coverage that you really don't need. Plus, policies available through an agent are generally more expensive than those available through direct writers or the Internet due to the cost of paying the agent's commission.

Finding a good agent is pretty much a hit and miss proposition. Your best bet is to rely on referrals from friends, neighbors, and family members who are happy with their insurance agent.

You can also consult your local phone book or do an Internet search to identify more names even though you won't have any information on their quality.

Keep in mind that there are actually two types of insurance agents: exclusive agents that represent only one company and independent agents that represent many companies. If you find an agent who works with only one company, you'll definitely want to check premium prices elsewhere before selecting an insurer to go with. And even if you're working with an independent agent who represents multiple companies, it still doesn't hurt to comparison shop with other agents or on the Internet to make sure you're getting the best deal possible.

Bottom line: If your preference is to have someone else do most of the legwork, an agent is your best bet, particularly if he has more than one company to choose from.

Direct Writers

Some insurance companies cut out the middle man (i.e., the agent) and instead employ their own salespeople who perform the agent's functions via phone. These companies are called direct writers. Shopping for a policy from a direct writer can be time consuming since you essentially have to call each company one by one to get a premium quote. At the same time though, some of the best deals can be found through direct writers due to their lower cost structure. You won't get quite the same personalized service as dealing with an agent, but the saving could make the impersonalization worth it to you.

Most direct writers advertise heavily in the mail, on the radio, and on television, so you've probably seen something from at least one of them without realizing you were being solicited by a direct writer. Also, some have started selling their policies through agents and then adding the agent's commission directly onto the premium you pay. Consult the Appendix for a list of websites operated by insurance companies some of which are direct writers.

The Internet

The Internet is a great place to do your comparison shopping. There are a large number of websites that can search through hundreds of insurers to find which ones offer the lowest premiums based on your specific situation. What's more, you can usually get a premium quote immediately after entering some information about yourself.Some insurance websites require you to give them a great deal of information up front such as your driver's license number, your social security number, the vehicle identification number (VIN#) of your vehicle, and information about any past accidents or traffic violations. This can be a lot of work, particularly if you do it for multiple policy searches. Other websites request only basic information in order to give you a ballpark quote. From there, you can decide if it's worth your time to enter all of the details required to get an actual quote.

If you want to get the rock bottom, lowest price possible on your auto insurance and you have the time to devote to it, the Internet is probably your best option. You won't have the comfort of consulting with an agent or even dealing with a salesperson. On the other hand, you'll be able to proceed at your own pace, from the comfort of your own home, without anyone pushing you to buy more.

Finding a website that sells auto insurance is extremely easy. All you have to do is put "auto insurance quotes" into a search engine and you'll get more than you can possibly use. For your convenience, we've also included the web address for some of the major online vendors of auto insurance in the Appendix of this publication.

In order to cut down on the time involved with shopping for insurance on the Internet, be sure to supply the most accurate information possible. Your driving record and the history of your vehicle will be scrutinized before a policy is issued, so it won't do you any good to try and skirt any blemishes. It will only make the process longer.

When shopping for an auto insurance policy, we recommend you follow these steps:

Step 1   Gather all of the personal information that will be needed in order to receive a premium quote. This includes your:

     – Driver's license number

     – Social security number

     – Vehicle make and model

     – Vehicle Identification number (VIN#) located on your registration or inside door panel

     – Driving history for the last five years, including any accidents or traffic citations

     – Policy limits and deductibles on your current auto policy

Step 2   Consult with your friends, neighbors, and family members to see who they use for their auto insurance and what their level of satisfaction has been.

Step 3   Decide which avenue(s) you'd like to use to shop for your new policy: an agent, a direct writer, or the Internet.

Step 4   Give some consideration to the types of coverage you are interested in purchasing as well as the policy limits for your liability coverage and the deductibles for your collision and comprehensive coverage. You can always request quotes for multiple options, but it's good to have an idea of what you want going in.

Step 5   Set aside some dedicated, uninterrupted time and contact the agents, companies, or websites you've decided to pursue. A good plan of action will help cut down on the amount of time involved.

Step 6   Take good notes so you can make sure you are getting "apples-to-apples" comparisons and so you will know who to contact if you should select a particular policy. There is a Premium Quote Comparison Worksheet in the Appendix to help you with this process.

Step 7   Narrow your list down to the least expensive two or three quotes and then take a look at those specific companies in more detail. Specifically, check:

– Each company's Weiss Safety Rating at www.weissratings.com to make sure the company is financially sound and will be around to pay your claim if you have one. See the Weiss Recommended Auto Insurers.

– Contact your state department of insurance to see if they can provide you with any information on the companies' history of consumer complaints or anything else that may aid you in your decision-making process.

– Conduct a search on the Internet using the company name. This may turn up postings from others that could be helpful to you.

Step 8   Select a company and submit an application to purchase your policy. If the paperwork comes back with a premium quote that differs from what you were originally quoted, don't hesitate about moving on to your second choice of companies.

Weiss Recommended Auto Insurers by State

The following pages list Weiss Recommended Auto Insurers (based strictly on financial safety) licensed to do business in each state. These insurers currently receive a Weiss Safety Rating of A+, A, A-, or B+, indicating their strong financial position. Companies are listed by their Safety Rating and then alphabetically within each Safety Rating grouping.

If an insurer is not on this list, it should not be automatically assumed that the firm is weak. Indeed, there are many firms that have not achieved a B+ or better rating but are in relatively good condition with adequate resources to cover their risk. Not being included in this list should not be construed as a recommendation to cancel a policy.

To get Weiss Safety Rating for a company not included here, go to www.weissratings.com.

Weiss Safety Rating	Our rating is measured on a scale from A to F and considers a wide range of factors. Highly rated companies are, in our opinion, less likely to experience financial difficulties than lower-rated firms. See "What Our Ratings Mean" in the Appendix for a definition of each rating category.
Name	The insurance company's legally registered name, which can sometimes differ from the name that the company uses for advertising. An insurer's name can be very similar to the name of other companies which may not be on this list, so make sure you note the exact name before contacting your agent.
City, Address, State	The address of the main office where you can contact the firm for additional information or for the location of local branches and/or registered agents.
Telephone	The telephone number to call for information on purchasing an insurance policy from the company.

The following list of recommended Auto Insurers by State is based on ratings as of the date of publication.

Alabama

A

Name	City	Address	State	Zip	Telephone
Ascot Surety & Casualty Company	Parker	10233 South Parker Road Suite	CO	80134	414-369-5033

A-

Name	City	Address	State	Zip	Telephone
Cincinnati Indemnity Co	Fairfield	6200 South Gilmore Road	OH	45014	414-369-5033

B+

Name	City	Address	State	Zip	Telephone
USAA General Indemnity Co	San Antonio	9800 Fredericksburg Road	TX	78288	414-369-5033
USAA Casualty Ins Co	San Antonio	9800 Fredericksburg Road	TX	78288	414-369-5033
Travelers Indemnity Co	Hartford	One Tower Square	CT	6183	414-369-5033
Travelers Casualty & Surety Co	Hartford	One Tower Square	CT	6183	414-369-5033
State Farm Mutual Automobile Ins Co	Bloomington	One State Farm Plaza	IL	61710	414-369-5033
State Farm Fire & Cas Co	Bloomington	One State Farm Plaza	IL	61710	414-369-5033
Sentry Ins A Mutual Co	Stevens Point	1800 North Point Drive	WI	54481	414-369-5033
Sentry Casualty Co	Stevens Point	1800 North Point Drive	WI	54481	414-369-5033
Securian Casualty Co	St. Paul	400 Robert Street North	MN	55101	414-369-5033
Owners Ins Co	Lima	2325 North Cole Street	OH	45801	414-369-5033
Home-Owners Ins Co	Lansing	6101 Anacapri Boulevard	MI	48917	414-369-5033
Geico General Ins Co	Omaha	3555 Farnam Street Suite 1440	NE	68131	414-369-5033
Frankenmuth Mutual Ins Co	Frankenmuth	One Mutual Avenue	MI	48787	414-369-5033
Country Mutual Ins Co	Bloomington	1701 Towanda Avenue	IL	61701	414-369-5033
Cincinnati Ins Co	Fairfield	6200 South Gilmore Road	OH	45014	414-369-5033
Auto-Owners Ins Co	Lansing	6101 Anacapri Boulevard	MI	48917	414-369-5033
Alfa Mutual Ins Co	Montgomery	2108 East South Boulevard	AL	36116	414-369-5033

Arizona

A+

Name	City	Address	State	Zip	Telephone
Copperpoint Mutual Ins Co	Phoenix	3030 N 3rd Street	AZ	85012	414-369-5033

A

Name	City	Address	State	Zip	Telephone
Ascot Surety & Casualty Company	Parker	10233 South Parker Road Suite	CO	80134	414-369-5033

Arizona (continued)

A-

Name	City	Address	State	Zip	Telephone
Cincinnati Indemnity Co	Fairfield	6200 South Gilmore Road	OH	45014	414-369-5033
Aca Financial Guaranty Corp	Baltimore	7 Saint Paul Street Suite 1660	MD	21202	414-369-5033

B+

Name	City	Address	State	Zip	Telephone
USAA General Indemnity Co	San Antonio	9800 Fredericksburg Road	TX	78288	414-369-5033
USAA Casualty Ins Co	San Antonio	9800 Fredericksburg Road	TX	78288	414-369-5033
Travelers Indemnity Co	Hartford	One Tower Square	CT	6183	414-369-5033
Travelers Casualty & Surety Co	Hartford	One Tower Square	CT	6183	414-369-5033
State Farm Mutual Automobile Ins Co	Bloomington	One State Farm Plaza	IL	61710	414-369-5033
State Farm Fire & Cas Co	Bloomington	One State Farm Plaza	IL	61710	414-369-5033
Sentry Ins A Mutual Co	Stevens Point	1800 North Point Drive	WI	54481	414-369-5033
Sentry Casualty Co	Stevens Point	1800 North Point Drive	WI	54481	414-369-5033
Securian Casualty Co	St. Paul	400 Robert Street North	MN	55101	414-369-5033
Owners Ins Co	Lima	2325 North Cole Street	OH	45801	414-369-5033
Geico General Ins Co	Omaha	3555 Farnam Street Suite 1440	NE	68131	414-369-5033
Frankenmuth Mutual Ins Co	Frankenmuth	One Mutual Avenue	MI	48787	414-369-5033
Country Mutual Ins Co	Bloomington	1701 Towanda Avenue	IL	61701	414-369-5033
Cincinnati Ins Co	Fairfield	6200 South Gilmore Road	OH	45014	414-369-5033
Auto-Owners Ins Co	Lansing	6101 Anacapri Boulevard	MI	48917	414-369-5033
American Standard Ins Co of WI	Madison	6000 American Parkway	WI	53783	414-369-5033
Acuity A Mutual Ins Co	Sheboygan	2800 South Taylor Drive	WI	53081	414-369-5033

Arkansas

A

Name	City	Address	State	Zip	Telephone
Ascot Surety & Casualty Company	Parker	10233 South Parker Road Suite	CO	80134	414-369-5033

A-

Name	City	Address	State	Zip	Telephone
Cincinnati Indemnity Co	Fairfield	6200 South Gilmore Road	OH	45014	414-369-5033
Aca Financial Guaranty Corp	Baltimore	7 Saint Paul Street Suite 1660	MD	21202	414-369-5033

B+

Name	City	Address	State	Zip	Telephone
USAA General Indemnity Co	San Antonio	9800 Fredericksburg Road	TX	78288	414-369-5033

Arkansas (continued)

B+

Name	City	Address	State	Zip	Telephone
USAA Casualty Ins Co	San Antonio	9800 Fredericksburg Road	TX	78288	414-369-5033
Travelers Indemnity Co	Hartford	One Tower Square	CT	6183	414-369-5033
Travelers Casualty & Surety Co	Hartford	One Tower Square	CT	6183	414-369-5033
State Farm Mutual Automobile Ins Co	Bloomington	One State Farm Plaza	IL	61710	414-369-5033
State Farm Fire & Cas Co	Bloomington	One State Farm Plaza	IL	61710	414-369-5033
Sentry Ins A Mutual Co	Stevens Point	1800 North Point Drive	WI	54481	414-369-5033
Sentry Casualty Co	Stevens Point	1800 North Point Drive	WI	54481	414-369-5033
Securian Casualty Co	St. Paul	400 Robert Street North	MN	55101	414-369-5033
Owners Ins Co	Lima	2325 North Cole Street	OH	45801	414-369-5033
Geico General Ins Co	Omaha	3555 Farnam Street Suite 1440	NE	68131	414-369-5033
Frankenmuth Mutual Ins Co	Frankenmuth	One Mutual Avenue	MI	48787	414-369-5033
Country Mutual Ins Co	Bloomington	1701 Towanda Avenue	IL	61701	414-369-5033
Cincinnati Ins Co	Fairfield	6200 South Gilmore Road	OH	45014	414-369-5033
Auto-Owners Ins Co	Lansing	6101 Anacapri Boulevard	MI	48917	414-369-5033

California

A-

Name	City	Address	State	Zip	Telephone
Cincinnati Indemnity Co	Fairfield	6200 South Gilmore Road	OH	45014	414-369-5033
Aca Financial Guaranty Corp	Baltimore	7 Saint Paul Street Suite 1660	MD	21202	414-369-5033

B+

Name	City	Address	State	Zip	Telephone
USAA General Indemnity Co	San Antonio	9800 Fredericksburg Road	TX	78288	414-369-5033
USAA Casualty Ins Co	San Antonio	9800 Fredericksburg Road	TX	78288	414-369-5033
Travelers Indemnity Co	Hartford	One Tower Square	CT	6183	414-369-5033
Travelers Casualty & Surety Co	Hartford	One Tower Square	CT	6183	414-369-5033
State Farm Mutual Automobile Ins Co	Bloomington	One State Farm Plaza	IL	61710	414-369-5033
State Farm Fire & Cas Co	Bloomington	One State Farm Plaza	IL	61710	414-369-5033
Sentry Ins A Mutual Co	Stevens Point	1800 North Point Drive	WI	54481	414-369-5033
Sentry Casualty Co	Stevens Point	1800 North Point Drive	WI	54481	414-369-5033
Securian Casualty Co	St. Paul	400 Robert Street North	MN	55101	414-369-5033
Interins Exchange	Costa Mesa	3333 Fairview Road	CA	92626	414-369-5033
Geico General Ins Co	Omaha	3555 Farnam Street Suite 1440	NE	68131	414-369-5033
Cincinnati Ins Co	Fairfield	6200 South Gilmore Road	OH	45014	414-369-5033

Colorado

A-

Name	City	Address	State	Zip	Telephone
Cincinnati Indemnity Co	Fairfield	6200 South Gilmore Road	OH	45014	414-369-5033

B+

Name	City	Address	State	Zip	Telephone
USAA General Indemnity Co	San Antonio	9800 Fredericksburg Road	TX	78288	414-369-5033
USAA Casualty Ins Co	San Antonio	9800 Fredericksburg Road	TX	78288	414-369-5033
Travelers Indemnity Co	Hartford	One Tower Square	CT	6183	414-369-5033
Travelers Casualty & Surety Co	Hartford	One Tower Square	CT	6183	414-369-5033
State Farm Mutual Automobile Ins Co	Bloomington	One State Farm Plaza	IL	61710	414-369-5033
State Farm Fire & Cas Co	Bloomington	One State Farm Plaza	IL	61710	414-369-5033
Sentry Ins A Mutual Co	Stevens Point	1800 North Point Drive	WI	54481	414-369-5033
Sentry Casualty Co	Stevens Point	1800 North Point Drive	WI	54481	414-369-5033
Securian Casualty Co	St. Paul	400 Robert Street North	MN	55101	414-369-5033
Owners Ins Co	Lima	2325 North Cole Street	OH	45801	414-369-5033
Home-Owners Ins Co	Lansing	6101 Anacapri Boulevard	MI	48917	414-369-5033
Geico General Ins Co	Omaha	3555 Farnam Street Suite 1440	NE	68131	414-369-5033
Country Mutual Ins Co	Bloomington	1701 Towanda Avenue	IL	61701	414-369-5033
Cincinnati Ins Co	Fairfield	6200 South Gilmore Road	OH	45014	414-369-5033
Auto-Owners Ins Co	Lansing	6101 Anacapri Boulevard	MI	48917	414-369-5033
American Standard Ins Co of WI	Madison	6000 American Parkway	WI	53783	414-369-5033
Acuity A Mutual Ins Co	Sheboygan	2800 South Taylor Drive	WI	53081	414-369-5033

Connecticut

A

Name	City	Address	State	Zip	Telephone
Ascot Surety & Casualty Company	Parker	10233 South Parker Road Suite	CO	80134	414-369-5033

A-

Name	City	Address	State	Zip	Telephone
Cincinnati Indemnity Co	Fairfield	6200 South Gilmore Road	OH	45014	414-369-5033

B+

Name	City	Address	State	Zip	Telephone
USAA General Indemnity Co	San Antonio	9800 Fredericksburg Road	TX	78288	414-369-5033
USAA Casualty Ins Co	San Antonio	9800 Fredericksburg Road	TX	78288	414-369-5033
Travelers Indemnity Co	Hartford	One Tower Square	CT	6183	414-369-5033

Connecticut (continued)

B+

Name	City	Address	State	Zip	Telephone
Travelers Casualty & Surety Co	Hartford	One Tower Square	CT	6183	414-369-5033
State Farm Mutual Automobile Ins Co	Bloomington	One State Farm Plaza	IL	61710	414-369-5033
State Farm Fire & Cas Co	Bloomington	One State Farm Plaza	IL	61710	414-369-5033
Sentry Ins A Mutual Co	Stevens Point	1800 North Point Drive	WI	54481	414-369-5033
Sentry Casualty Co	Stevens Point	1800 North Point Drive	WI	54481	414-369-5033
Securian Casualty Co	St. Paul	400 Robert Street North	MN	55101	414-369-5033
Geico General Ins Co	Omaha	3555 Farnam Street Suite 1440	NE	68131	414-369-5033
Frankenmuth Mutual Ins Co	Frankenmuth	One Mutual Avenue	MI	48787	414-369-5033
Farm Family Casualty Ins Co	Glenmont	344 Route 9w	NY	12077	414-369-5033
Country Mutual Ins Co	Bloomington	1701 Towanda Avenue	IL	61701	414-369-5033
Cincinnati Ins Co	Fairfield	6200 South Gilmore Road	OH	45014	414-369-5033

Delaware

A+

Name	City	Address	State	Zip	Telephone
Nuclear Electric Ins Ltd	Wilmington	1201 Market St Ste 1200	DE	19801	414-369-5033

A

Name	City	Address	State	Zip	Telephone
Ascot Surety & Casualty Company	Parker	10233 South Parker Road Suite	CO	80134	414-369-5033

A-

Name	City	Address	State	Zip	Telephone
Cincinnati Indemnity Co	Fairfield	6200 South Gilmore Road	OH	45014	414-369-5033

B+

Name	City	Address	State	Zip	Telephone
USAA General Indemnity Co	San Antonio	9800 Fredericksburg Road	TX	78288	414-369-5033
USAA Casualty Ins Co	San Antonio	9800 Fredericksburg Road	TX	78288	414-369-5033
Travelers Indemnity Co	Hartford	One Tower Square	CT	6183	414-369-5033
Travelers Casualty & Surety Co	Hartford	One Tower Square	CT	6183	414-369-5033
State Farm Mutual Automobile Ins Co	Bloomington	One State Farm Plaza	IL	61710	414-369-5033
State Farm Fire & Cas Co	Bloomington	One State Farm Plaza	IL	61710	414-369-5033
Sentry Ins A Mutual Co	Stevens Point	1800 North Point Drive	WI	54481	414-369-5033
Sentry Casualty Co	Stevens Point	1800 North Point Drive	WI	54481	414-369-5033
Securian Casualty Co	St. Paul	400 Robert Street North	MN	55101	414-369-5033

Delaware (continued)

B+

Name	City	Address	State	Zip	Telephone
Geico General Ins Co	Omaha	3555 Farnam Street Suite 1440	NE	68131	414-369-5033
Farm Family Casualty Ins Co	Glenmont	344 Route 9w	NY	12077	414-369-5033
Country Mutual Ins Co	Bloomington	1701 Towanda Avenue	IL	61701	414-369-5033
Cincinnati Ins Co	Fairfield	6200 South Gilmore Road	OH	45014	414-369-5033

District of Columbia

A

Name	City	Address	State	Zip	Telephone
Ascot Surety & Casualty Company	Parker	10233 South Parker Road Suite	CO	80134	414-369-5033

A-

Name	City	Address	State	Zip	Telephone
Cincinnati Indemnity Co	Fairfield	6200 South Gilmore Road	OH	45014	414-369-5033

B+

Name	City	Address	State	Zip	Telephone
USAA General Indemnity Co	San Antonio	9800 Fredericksburg Road	TX	78288	414-369-5033
USAA Casualty Ins Co	San Antonio	9800 Fredericksburg Road	TX	78288	414-369-5033
Travelers Indemnity Co	Hartford	One Tower Square	CT	6183	414-369-5033
Travelers Casualty & Surety Co	Hartford	One Tower Square	CT	6183	414-369-5033
State Farm Mutual Automobile Ins Co	Bloomington	One State Farm Plaza	IL	61710	414-369-5033
State Farm Fire & Cas Co	Bloomington	One State Farm Plaza	IL	61710	414-369-5033
Sentry Ins A Mutual Co	Stevens Point	1800 North Point Drive	WI	54481	414-369-5033
Sentry Casualty Co	Stevens Point	1800 North Point Drive	WI	54481	414-369-5033
Securian Casualty Co	St. Paul	400 Robert Street North	MN	55101	414-369-5033
Geico General Ins Co	Omaha	3555 Farnam Street Suite 1440	NE	68131	414-369-5033
Cincinnati Ins Co	Fairfield	6200 South Gilmore Road	OH	45014	414-369-5033

Florida

A

Name	City	Address	State	Zip	Telephone
Ascot Surety & Casualty Company	Parker	10233 South Parker Road Suite	CO	80134	414-369-5033

Florida (continued)

A-

Name	City	Address	State	Zip	Telephone
Cincinnati Indemnity Co	Fairfield	6200 South Gilmore Road	OH	45014	414-369-5033
Asi Preferred Ins Corp	St. Petersburg	1 Asi Way	FL	33702	414-369-5033
Aca Financial Guaranty Corp	Baltimore	7 Saint Paul Street Suite 1660	MD	21202	414-369-5033

B+

Name	City	Address	State	Zip	Telephone
USAA General Indemnity Co	San Antonio	9800 Fredericksburg Road	TX	78288	414-369-5033
USAA Casualty Ins Co	San Antonio	9800 Fredericksburg Road	TX	78288	414-369-5033
Travelers Indemnity Co	Hartford	One Tower Square	CT	6183	414-369-5033
Travelers Casualty & Surety Co	Hartford	One Tower Square	CT	6183	414-369-5033
State Farm Mutual Automobile Ins Co	Bloomington	One State Farm Plaza	IL	61710	414-369-5033
State Farm Fire & Cas Co	Bloomington	One State Farm Plaza	IL	61710	414-369-5033
Sentry Ins A Mutual Co	Stevens Point	1800 North Point Drive	WI	54481	414-369-5033
Sentry Casualty Co	Stevens Point	1800 North Point Drive	WI	54481	414-369-5033
Securian Casualty Co	St. Paul	400 Robert Street North	MN	55101	414-369-5033
Owners Ins Co	Lima	2325 North Cole Street	OH	45801	414-369-5033
Geico General Ins Co	Omaha	3555 Farnam Street Suite 1440	NE	68131	414-369-5033
Frankenmuth Mutual Ins Co	Frankenmuth	One Mutual Avenue	MI	48787	414-369-5033
Country Mutual Ins Co	Bloomington	1701 Towanda Avenue	IL	61701	414-369-5033
Cooperativa D Seguros Multiples D Pr	San Juan	38 Nevarez Street	PR	00927	414-369-5033
Cincinnati Ins Co	Fairfield	6200 South Gilmore Road	OH	45014	414-369-5033
Auto-Owners Ins Co	Lansing	6101 Anacapri Boulevard	MI	48917	414-369-5033
Acuity A Mutual Ins Co	Sheboygan	2800 South Taylor Drive	WI	53081	414-369-5033

Georgia

A

Name	City	Address	State	Zip	Telephone
Ascot Surety & Casualty Company	Parker	10233 South Parker Road Suite	CO	80134	414-369-5033

A-

Name	City	Address	State	Zip	Telephone
Cincinnati Indemnity Co	Fairfield	6200 South Gilmore Road	OH	45014	414-369-5033
Aca Financial Guaranty Corp	Baltimore	7 Saint Paul Street Suite 1660	MD	21202	414-369-5033

Georgia (continued)

B+

Name	City	Address	State	Zip	Telephone
USAA General Indemnity Co	San Antonio	9800 Fredericksburg Road	TX	78288	414-369-5033
USAA Casualty Ins Co	San Antonio	9800 Fredericksburg Road	TX	78288	414-369-5033
Travelers Indemnity Co	Hartford	One Tower Square	CT	6183	414-369-5033
Travelers Casualty & Surety Co	Hartford	One Tower Square	CT	6183	414-369-5033
State Farm Mutual Automobile Ins Co	Bloomington	One State Farm Plaza	IL	61710	414-369-5033
State Farm Fire & Cas Co	Bloomington	One State Farm Plaza	IL	61710	414-369-5033
Sentry Ins A Mutual Co	Stevens Point	1800 North Point Drive	WI	54481	414-369-5033
Sentry Casualty Co	Stevens Point	1800 North Point Drive	WI	54481	414-369-5033
Securian Casualty Co	St. Paul	400 Robert Street North	MN	55101	414-369-5033
Property-Owners Ins Co	Marion	3950 West Delphi Pike	IN	46952	414-369-5033
Owners Ins Co	Lima	2325 North Cole Street	OH	45801	414-369-5033
Home-Owners Ins Co	Lansing	6101 Anacapri Boulevard	MI	48917	414-369-5033
Geico General Ins Co	Omaha	3555 Farnam Street Suite 1440	NE	68131	414-369-5033
Frankenmuth Mutual Ins Co	Frankenmuth	One Mutual Avenue	MI	48787	414-369-5033
Country Mutual Ins Co	Bloomington	1701 Towanda Avenue	IL	61701	414-369-5033
Cincinnati Ins Co	Fairfield	6200 South Gilmore Road	OH	45014	414-369-5033
Auto-Owners Ins Co	Lansing	6101 Anacapri Boulevard	MI	48917	414-369-5033

Hawaii

A-

Name	City	Address	State	Zip	Telephone
Cincinnati Indemnity Co	Fairfield	6200 South Gilmore Road	OH	45014	414-369-5033

B+

Name	City	Address	State	Zip	Telephone
USAA General Indemnity Co	San Antonio	9800 Fredericksburg Road	TX	78288	414-369-5033
USAA Casualty Ins Co	San Antonio	9800 Fredericksburg Road	TX	78288	414-369-5033
Travelers Indemnity Co	Hartford	One Tower Square	CT	6183	414-369-5033
Travelers Casualty & Surety Co	Hartford	One Tower Square	CT	6183	414-369-5033
State Farm Mutual Automobile Ins Co	Bloomington	One State Farm Plaza	IL	61710	414-369-5033
State Farm Fire & Cas Co	Bloomington	One State Farm Plaza	IL	61710	414-369-5033
Sentry Ins A Mutual Co	Stevens Point	1800 North Point Drive	WI	54481	414-369-5033
Sentry Casualty Co	Stevens Point	1800 North Point Drive	WI	54481	414-369-5033
Securian Casualty Co	St. Paul	400 Robert Street North	MN	55101	414-369-5033
Interins Exchange	Costa Mesa	3333 Fairview Road	CA	92626	414-369-5033

Hawaii (continued)

B+

Name	City	Address	State	Zip	Telephone
Cincinnati Ins Co	Fairfield	6200 South Gilmore Road	OH	45014	414-369-5033

Idaho

A

Name	City	Address	State	Zip	Telephone
Ascot Surety & Casualty Company	Parker	10233 South Parker Road Suite	CO	80134	414-369-5033

A-

Name	City	Address	State	Zip	Telephone
Cincinnati Indemnity Co	Fairfield	6200 South Gilmore Road	OH	45014	414-369-5033

B+

Name	City	Address	State	Zip	Telephone
USAA General Indemnity Co	San Antonio	9800 Fredericksburg Road	TX	78288	414-369-5033
USAA Casualty Ins Co	San Antonio	9800 Fredericksburg Road	TX	78288	414-369-5033
Travelers Indemnity Co	Hartford	One Tower Square	CT	6183	414-369-5033
Travelers Casualty & Surety Co	Hartford	One Tower Square	CT	6183	414-369-5033
State Farm Mutual Automobile Ins Co	Bloomington	One State Farm Plaza	IL	61710	414-369-5033
State Farm Fire & Cas Co	Bloomington	One State Farm Plaza	IL	61710	414-369-5033
Sentry Ins A Mutual Co	Stevens Point	1800 North Point Drive	WI	54481	414-369-5033
Sentry Casualty Co	Stevens Point	1800 North Point Drive	WI	54481	414-369-5033
Securian Casualty Co	St. Paul	400 Robert Street North	MN	55101	414-369-5033
Owners Ins Co	Lima	2325 North Cole Street	OH	45801	414-369-5033
Geico General Ins Co	Omaha	3555 Farnam Street Suite 1440	NE	68131	414-369-5033
Country Mutual Ins Co	Bloomington	1701 Towanda Avenue	IL	61701	414-369-5033
Cincinnati Ins Co	Fairfield	6200 South Gilmore Road	OH	45014	414-369-5033
Auto-Owners Ins Co	Lansing	6101 Anacapri Boulevard	MI	48917	414-369-5033
American Standard Ins Co of WI	Madison	6000 American Parkway	WI	53783	414-369-5033
Acuity A Mutual Ins Co	Sheboygan	2800 South Taylor Drive	WI	53081	414-369-5033

Illinois

A-

Name	City	Address	State	Zip	Telephone
Cincinnati Indemnity Co	Fairfield	6200 South Gilmore Road	OH	45014	414-369-5033
Aca Financial Guaranty Corp	Baltimore	7 Saint Paul Street Suite 1660	MD	21202	414-369-5033

Illinois (continued)

B+

Name	City	Address	State	Zip	Telephone
USAA General Indemnity Co	San Antonio	9800 Fredericksburg Road	TX	78288	414-369-5033
USAA Casualty Ins Co	San Antonio	9800 Fredericksburg Road	TX	78288	414-369-5033
Travelers Indemnity Co	Hartford	One Tower Square	CT	6183	414-369-5033
Travelers Casualty & Surety Co	Hartford	One Tower Square	CT	6183	414-369-5033
State Farm Mutual Automobile Ins Co	Bloomington	One State Farm Plaza	IL	61710	414-369-5033
State Farm Fire & Cas Co	Bloomington	One State Farm Plaza	IL	61710	414-369-5033
Sentry Ins A Mutual Co	Stevens Point	1800 North Point Drive	WI	54481	414-369-5033
Sentry Casualty Co	Stevens Point	1800 North Point Drive	WI	54481	414-369-5033
Securian Casualty Co	St. Paul	400 Robert Street North	MN	55101	414-369-5033
Owners Ins Co	Lima	2325 North Cole Street	OH	45801	414-369-5033
Home-Owners Ins Co	Lansing	6101 Anacapri Boulevard	MI	48917	414-369-5033
Geico General Ins Co	Omaha	3555 Farnam Street Suite 1440	NE	68131	414-369-5033
Frankenmuth Mutual Ins Co	Frankenmuth	One Mutual Avenue	MI	48787	414-369-5033
Country Mutual Ins Co	Bloomington	1701 Towanda Avenue	IL	61701	414-369-5033
Cincinnati Ins Co	Fairfield	6200 South Gilmore Road	OH	45014	414-369-5033
Auto-Owners Ins Co	Lansing	6101 Anacapri Boulevard	MI	48917	414-369-5033
American Standard Ins Co of WI	Madison	6000 American Parkway	WI	53783	414-369-5033
Acuity A Mutual Ins Co	Sheboygan	2800 South Taylor Drive	WI	53081	414-369-5033

Indiana

A

Name	City	Address	State	Zip	Telephone
Ascot Surety & Casualty Company	Parker	10233 South Parker Road Suite	CO	80134	414-369-5033

A-

Name	City	Address	State	Zip	Telephone
Cincinnati Indemnity Co	Fairfield	6200 South Gilmore Road	OH	45014	414-369-5033

B+

Name	City	Address	State	Zip	Telephone
USAA General Indemnity Co	San Antonio	9800 Fredericksburg Road	TX	78288	414-369-5033
USAA Casualty Ins Co	San Antonio	9800 Fredericksburg Road	TX	78288	414-369-5033
Travelers Indemnity Co	Hartford	One Tower Square	CT	6183	414-369-5033
Travelers Casualty & Surety Co	Hartford	One Tower Square	CT	6183	414-369-5033
State Farm Mutual Automobile Ins Co	Bloomington	One State Farm Plaza	IL	61710	414-369-5033

Indiana (continued)

B+

Name	City	Address	State	Zip	Telephone
State Farm Fire & Cas Co	Bloomington	One State Farm Plaza	IL	61710	414-369-5033
Sentry Ins A Mutual Co	Stevens Point	1800 North Point Drive	WI	54481	414-369-5033
Sentry Casualty Co	Stevens Point	1800 North Point Drive	WI	54481	414-369-5033
Securian Casualty Co	St. Paul	400 Robert Street North	MN	55101	414-369-5033
Property-Owners Ins Co	Marion	3950 West Delphi Pike	IN	46952	414-369-5033
Owners Ins Co	Lima	2325 North Cole Street	OH	45801	414-369-5033
Motorists Mutual Ins Co	Columbus	471 East Broad Street	OH	43215	414-369-5033
Geico General Ins Co	Omaha	3555 Farnam Street Suite 1440	NE	68131	414-369-5033
Frankenmuth Mutual Ins Co	Frankenmuth	One Mutual Avenue	MI	48787	414-369-5033
Country Mutual Ins Co	Bloomington	1701 Towanda Avenue	IL	61701	414-369-5033
Cincinnati Ins Co	Fairfield	6200 South Gilmore Road	OH	45014	414-369-5033
Auto-Owners Ins Co	Lansing	6101 Anacapri Boulevard	MI	48917	414-369-5033
American Standard Ins Co of WI	Madison	6000 American Parkway	WI	53783	414-369-5033
Acuity A Mutual Ins Co	Sheboygan	2800 South Taylor Drive	WI	53081	414-369-5033

Iowa

A-

Name	City	Address	State	Zip	Telephone
Cincinnati Indemnity Co	Fairfield	6200 South Gilmore Road	OH	45014	414-369-5033

B+

Name	City	Address	State	Zip	Telephone
USAA General Indemnity Co	San Antonio	9800 Fredericksburg Road	TX	78288	414-369-5033
USAA Casualty Ins Co	San Antonio	9800 Fredericksburg Road	TX	78288	414-369-5033
Travelers Indemnity Co	Hartford	One Tower Square	CT	6183	414-369-5033
Travelers Casualty & Surety Co	Hartford	One Tower Square	CT	6183	414-369-5033
State Farm Mutual Automobile Ins Co	Bloomington	One State Farm Plaza	IL	61710	414-369-5033
State Farm Fire & Cas Co	Bloomington	One State Farm Plaza	IL	61710	414-369-5033
Sentry Ins A Mutual Co	Stevens Point	1800 North Point Drive	WI	54481	414-369-5033
Sentry Casualty Co	Stevens Point	1800 North Point Drive	WI	54481	414-369-5033
Securian Casualty Co	St. Paul	400 Robert Street North	MN	55101	414-369-5033
Owners Ins Co	Lima	2325 North Cole Street	OH	45801	414-369-5033
Geico General Ins Co	Omaha	3555 Farnam Street Suite 1440	NE	68131	414-369-5033
Frankenmuth Mutual Ins Co	Frankenmuth	One Mutual Avenue	MI	48787	414-369-5033
Country Mutual Ins Co	Bloomington	1701 Towanda Avenue	IL	61701	414-369-5033

Iowa (continued)

B+

Name	City	Address	State	Zip	Telephone
Cincinnati Ins Co	Fairfield	6200 South Gilmore Road	OH	45014	414-369-5033
Auto-Owners Ins Co	Lansing	6101 Anacapri Boulevard	MI	48917	414-369-5033
American Standard Ins Co of WI	Madison	6000 American Parkway	WI	53783	414-369-5033
Acuity A Mutual Ins Co	Sheboygan	2800 South Taylor Drive	WI	53081	414-369-5033

Kansas

A

Name	City	Address	State	Zip	Telephone
Ascot Surety & Casualty Company	Parker	10233 South Parker Road Suite	CO	80134	414-369-5033

A-

Name	City	Address	State	Zip	Telephone
Cincinnati Indemnity Co	Fairfield	6200 South Gilmore Road	OH	45014	414-369-5033

B+

Name	City	Address	State	Zip	Telephone
USAA General Indemnity Co	San Antonio	9800 Fredericksburg Road	TX	78288	414-369-5033
USAA Casualty Ins Co	San Antonio	9800 Fredericksburg Road	TX	78288	414-369-5033
Travelers Indemnity Co	Hartford	One Tower Square	CT	6183	414-369-5033
Travelers Casualty & Surety Co	Hartford	One Tower Square	CT	6183	414-369-5033
State Farm Mutual Automobile Ins Co	Bloomington	One State Farm Plaza	IL	61710	414-369-5033
State Farm Fire & Cas Co	Bloomington	One State Farm Plaza	IL	61710	414-369-5033
Sentry Ins A Mutual Co	Stevens Point	1800 North Point Drive	WI	54481	414-369-5033
Sentry Casualty Co	Stevens Point	1800 North Point Drive	WI	54481	414-369-5033
Securian Casualty Co	St. Paul	400 Robert Street North	MN	55101	414-369-5033
Owners Ins Co	Lima	2325 North Cole Street	OH	45801	414-369-5033
Geico General Ins Co	Omaha	3555 Farnam Street Suite 1440	NE	68131	414-369-5033
Frankenmuth Mutual Ins Co	Frankenmuth	One Mutual Avenue	MI	48787	414-369-5033
Country Mutual Ins Co	Bloomington	1701 Towanda Avenue	IL	61701	414-369-5033
Cincinnati Ins Co	Fairfield	6200 South Gilmore Road	OH	45014	414-369-5033
Auto-Owners Ins Co	Lansing	6101 Anacapri Boulevard	MI	48917	414-369-5033
American Standard Ins Co of WI	Madison	6000 American Parkway	WI	53783	414-369-5033
Acuity A Mutual Ins Co	Sheboygan	2800 South Taylor Drive	WI	53081	414-369-5033

Kentucky

A

Name	City	Address	State	Zip	Telephone
Ascot Surety & Casualty Company	Parker	10233 South Parker Road Suite	CO	80134	414-369-5033

A-

Name	City	Address	State	Zip	Telephone
Cincinnati Indemnity Co	Fairfield	6200 South Gilmore Road	OH	45014	414-369-5033

B+

Name	City	Address	State	Zip	Telephone
USAA General Indemnity Co	San Antonio	9800 Fredericksburg Road	TX	78288	414-369-5033
USAA Casualty Ins Co	San Antonio	9800 Fredericksburg Road	TX	78288	414-369-5033
Travelers Indemnity Co	Hartford	One Tower Square	CT	6183	414-369-5033
Travelers Casualty & Surety Co	Hartford	One Tower Square	CT	6183	414-369-5033
State Farm Mutual Automobile Ins Co	Bloomington	One State Farm Plaza	IL	61710	414-369-5033
State Farm Fire & Cas Co	Bloomington	One State Farm Plaza	IL	61710	414-369-5033
Sentry Ins A Mutual Co	Stevens Point	1800 North Point Drive	WI	54481	414-369-5033
Sentry Casualty Co	Stevens Point	1800 North Point Drive	WI	54481	414-369-5033
Securian Casualty Co	St. Paul	400 Robert Street North	MN	55101	414-369-5033
Owners Ins Co	Lima	2325 North Cole Street	OH	45801	414-369-5033
Motorists Mutual Ins Co	Columbus	471 East Broad Street	OH	43215	414-369-5033
Geico General Ins Co	Omaha	3555 Farnam Street Suite 1440	NE	68131	414-369-5033
Frankenmuth Mutual Ins Co	Frankenmuth	One Mutual Avenue	MI	48787	414-369-5033
Country Mutual Ins Co	Bloomington	1701 Towanda Avenue	IL	61701	414-369-5033
Cincinnati Ins Co	Fairfield	6200 South Gilmore Road	OH	45014	414-369-5033
Auto-Owners Ins Co	Lansing	6101 Anacapri Boulevard	MI	48917	414-369-5033
Acuity A Mutual Ins Co	Sheboygan	2800 South Taylor Drive	WI	53081	414-369-5033

Louisiana

A

Name	City	Address	State	Zip	Telephone
Ascot Surety & Casualty Company	Parker	10233 South Parker Road Suite	CO	80134	414-369-5033

A-

Name	City	Address	State	Zip	Telephone
Cincinnati Indemnity Co	Fairfield	6200 South Gilmore Road	OH	45014	414-369-5033
Aca Financial Guaranty Corp	Baltimore	7 Saint Paul Street Suite 1660	MD	21202	414-369-5033

Louisiana (continued)

B+

Name	City	Address	State	Zip	Telephone
USAA General Indemnity Co	San Antonio	9800 Fredericksburg Road	TX	78288	414-369-5033
USAA Casualty Ins Co	San Antonio	9800 Fredericksburg Road	TX	78288	414-369-5033
Travelers Indemnity Co	Hartford	One Tower Square	CT	6183	414-369-5033
Travelers Casualty & Surety Co	Hartford	One Tower Square	CT	6183	414-369-5033
State Farm Mutual Automobile Ins Co	Bloomington	One State Farm Plaza	IL	61710	414-369-5033
State Farm Fire & Cas Co	Bloomington	One State Farm Plaza	IL	61710	414-369-5033
Sentry Ins A Mutual Co	Stevens Point	1800 North Point Drive	WI	54481	414-369-5033
Sentry Casualty Co	Stevens Point	1800 North Point Drive	WI	54481	414-369-5033
Securian Casualty Co	St. Paul	400 Robert Street North	MN	55101	414-369-5033
Geico General Ins Co	Omaha	3555 Farnam Street Suite 1440	NE	68131	414-369-5033
Cincinnati Ins Co	Fairfield	6200 South Gilmore Road	OH	45014	414-369-5033

Maine

A

Name	City	Address	State	Zip	Telephone
Ascot Surety & Casualty Company	Parker	10233 South Parker Road Suite	CO	80134	414-369-5033

A-

Name	City	Address	State	Zip	Telephone
Cincinnati Indemnity Co	Fairfield	6200 South Gilmore Road	OH	45014	414-369-5033

B+

Name	City	Address	State	Zip	Telephone
USAA General Indemnity Co	San Antonio	9800 Fredericksburg Road	TX	78288	414-369-5033
USAA Casualty Ins Co	San Antonio	9800 Fredericksburg Road	TX	78288	414-369-5033
Travelers Indemnity Co	Hartford	One Tower Square	CT	6183	414-369-5033
Travelers Casualty & Surety Co	Hartford	One Tower Square	CT	6183	414-369-5033
State Farm Mutual Automobile Ins Co	Bloomington	One State Farm Plaza	IL	61710	414-369-5033
State Farm Fire & Cas Co	Bloomington	One State Farm Plaza	IL	61710	414-369-5033
Sentry Ins A Mutual Co	Stevens Point	1800 North Point Drive	WI	54481	414-369-5033
Sentry Casualty Co	Stevens Point	1800 North Point Drive	WI	54481	414-369-5033
Securian Casualty Co	St. Paul	400 Robert Street North	MN	55101	414-369-5033
Interins Exchange	Costa Mesa	3333 Fairview Road	CA	92626	414-369-5033
Geico General Ins Co	Omaha	3555 Farnam Street Suite 1440	NE	68131	414-369-5033
Frankenmuth Mutual Ins Co	Frankenmuth	One Mutual Avenue	MI	48787	414-369-5033

Maine (continued)

B+

Name	City	Address	State	Zip	Telephone
Farm Family Casualty Ins Co	Glenmont	344 Route 9w	NY	12077	414-369-5033
Country Mutual Ins Co	Bloomington	1701 Towanda Avenue	IL	61701	414-369-5033
Cincinnati Ins Co	Fairfield	6200 South Gilmore Road	OH	45014	414-369-5033
Acuity A Mutual Ins Co	Sheboygan	2800 South Taylor Drive	WI	53081	414-369-5033

Maryland

A-

Name	City	Address	State	Zip	Telephone
Cincinnati Indemnity Co	Fairfield	6200 South Gilmore Road	OH	45014	414-369-5033

B+

Name	City	Address	State	Zip	Telephone
USAA General Indemnity Co	San Antonio	9800 Fredericksburg Road	TX	78288	414-369-5033
USAA Casualty Ins Co	San Antonio	9800 Fredericksburg Road	TX	78288	414-369-5033
Travelers Indemnity Co	Hartford	One Tower Square	CT	6183	414-369-5033
Travelers Casualty & Surety Co	Hartford	One Tower Square	CT	6183	414-369-5033
State Farm Mutual Automobile Ins Co	Bloomington	One State Farm Plaza	IL	61710	414-369-5033
State Farm Fire & Cas Co	Bloomington	One State Farm Plaza	IL	61710	414-369-5033
Sentry Ins A Mutual Co	Stevens Point	1800 North Point Drive	WI	54481	414-369-5033
Sentry Casualty Co	Stevens Point	1800 North Point Drive	WI	54481	414-369-5033
Securian Casualty Co	St. Paul	400 Robert Street North	MN	55101	414-369-5033
Geico General Ins Co	Omaha	3555 Farnam Street Suite 1440	NE	68131	414-369-5033
Frankenmuth Mutual Ins Co	Frankenmuth	One Mutual Avenue	MI	48787	414-369-5033
Farm Family Casualty Ins Co	Glenmont	344 Route 9w	NY	12077	414-369-5033
Country Mutual Ins Co	Bloomington	1701 Towanda Avenue	IL	61701	414-369-5033
Cincinnati Ins Co	Fairfield	6200 South Gilmore Road	OH	45014	414-369-5033

Massachusetts

A

Name	City	Address	State	Zip	Telephone
Ascot Surety & Casualty Company	Parker	10233 South Parker Road Suite	CO	80134	414-369-5033

A-

Name	City	Address	State	Zip	Telephone
Cincinnati Indemnity Co	Fairfield	6200 South Gilmore Road	OH	45014	414-369-5033

Massachusetts (continued)

A-

Name	City	Address	State	Zip	Telephone
Asi Preferred Ins Corp	St. Petersburg	1 Asi Way	FL	33702	414-369-5033

B+

Name	City	Address	State	Zip	Telephone
USAA General Indemnity Co	San Antonio	9800 Fredericksburg Road	TX	78288	414-369-5033
USAA Casualty Ins Co	San Antonio	9800 Fredericksburg Road	TX	78288	414-369-5033
Travelers Indemnity Co	Hartford	One Tower Square	CT	6183	414-369-5033
Travelers Casualty & Surety Co	Hartford	One Tower Square	CT	6183	414-369-5033
State Farm Mutual Automobile Ins Co	Bloomington	One State Farm Plaza	IL	61710	414-369-5033
State Farm Fire & Cas Co	Bloomington	One State Farm Plaza	IL	61710	414-369-5033
Sentry Ins A Mutual Co	Stevens Point	1800 North Point Drive	WI	54481	414-369-5033
Sentry Casualty Co	Stevens Point	1800 North Point Drive	WI	54481	414-369-5033
Securian Casualty Co	St. Paul	400 Robert Street North	MN	55101	414-369-5033
Geico General Ins Co	Omaha	3555 Farnam Street Suite 1440	NE	68131	414-369-5033
Frankenmuth Mutual Ins Co	Frankenmuth	One Mutual Avenue	MI	48787	414-369-5033
Farm Family Casualty Ins Co	Glenmont	344 Route 9w	NY	12077	414-369-5033
Country Mutual Ins Co	Bloomington	1701 Towanda Avenue	IL	61701	414-369-5033
Cincinnati Ins Co	Fairfield	6200 South Gilmore Road	OH	45014	414-369-5033

Michigan

A-

Name	City	Address	State	Zip	Telephone
Cincinnati Indemnity Co	Fairfield	6200 South Gilmore Road	OH	45014	414-369-5033

B+

Name	City	Address	State	Zip	Telephone
USAA General Indemnity Co	San Antonio	9800 Fredericksburg Road	TX	78288	414-369-5033
USAA Casualty Ins Co	San Antonio	9800 Fredericksburg Road	TX	78288	414-369-5033
Travelers Indemnity Co	Hartford	One Tower Square	CT	6183	414-369-5033
Travelers Casualty & Surety Co	Hartford	One Tower Square	CT	6183	414-369-5033
State Farm Mutual Automobile Ins Co	Bloomington	One State Farm Plaza	IL	61710	414-369-5033
State Farm Fire & Cas Co	Bloomington	One State Farm Plaza	IL	61710	414-369-5033
Sentry Ins A Mutual Co	Stevens Point	1800 North Point Drive	WI	54481	414-369-5033
Sentry Casualty Co	Stevens Point	1800 North Point Drive	WI	54481	414-369-5033
Securian Casualty Co	St. Paul	400 Robert Street North	MN	55101	414-369-5033

Michigan (continued)

B+

Name	City	Address	State	Zip	Telephone
Property-Owners Ins Co	Marion	3950 West Delphi Pike	IN	46952	414-369-5033
Motorists Mutual Ins Co	Columbus	471 East Broad Street	OH	43215	414-369-5033
Home-Owners Ins Co	Lansing	6101 Anacapri Boulevard	MI	48917	414-369-5033
Frankenmuth Mutual Ins Co	Frankenmuth	One Mutual Avenue	MI	48787	414-369-5033
Country Mutual Ins Co	Bloomington	1701 Towanda Avenue	IL	61701	414-369-5033
Cincinnati Ins Co	Fairfield	6200 South Gilmore Road	OH	45014	414-369-5033
Auto-Owners Ins Co	Lansing	6101 Anacapri Boulevard	MI	48917	414-369-5033
Acuity A Mutual Ins Co	Sheboygan	2800 South Taylor Drive	WI	53081	414-369-5033

Minnesota

A

Name	City	Address	State	Zip	Telephone
Ascot Surety & Casualty Company	Parker	10233 South Parker Road Suite	CO	80134	414-369-5033

A-

Name	City	Address	State	Zip	Telephone
Cincinnati Indemnity Co	Fairfield	6200 South Gilmore Road	OH	45014	414-369-5033
Aca Financial Guaranty Corp	Baltimore	7 Saint Paul Street Suite 1660	MD	21202	414-369-5033

B+

Name	City	Address	State	Zip	Telephone
USAA General Indemnity Co	San Antonio	9800 Fredericksburg Road	TX	78288	414-369-5033
USAA Casualty Ins Co	San Antonio	9800 Fredericksburg Road	TX	78288	414-369-5033
Travelers Indemnity Co	Hartford	One Tower Square	CT	6183	414-369-5033
Travelers Casualty & Surety Co	Hartford	One Tower Square	CT	6183	414-369-5033
State Farm Mutual Automobile Ins Co	Bloomington	One State Farm Plaza	IL	61710	414-369-5033
State Farm Fire & Cas Co	Bloomington	One State Farm Plaza	IL	61710	414-369-5033
Sentry Ins A Mutual Co	Stevens Point	1800 North Point Drive	WI	54481	414-369-5033
Sentry Casualty Co	Stevens Point	1800 North Point Drive	WI	54481	414-369-5033
Securian Casualty Co	St. Paul	400 Robert Street North	MN	55101	414-369-5033
Owners Ins Co	Lima	2325 North Cole Street	OH	45801	414-369-5033
Geico General Ins Co	Omaha	3555 Farnam Street Suite 1440	NE	68131	414-369-5033
Frankenmuth Mutual Ins Co	Frankenmuth	One Mutual Avenue	MI	48787	414-369-5033
Country Mutual Ins Co	Bloomington	1701 Towanda Avenue	IL	61701	414-369-5033
Cincinnati Ins Co	Fairfield	6200 South Gilmore Road	OH	45014	414-369-5033

Minnesota (continued)

B+

Name	City	Address	State	Zip	Telephone
Auto-Owners Ins Co	Lansing	6101 Anacapri Boulevard	MI	48917	414-369-5033
American Standard Ins Co of WI	Madison	6000 American Parkway	WI	53783	414-369-5033
Acuity A Mutual Ins Co	Sheboygan	2800 South Taylor Drive	WI	53081	414-369-5033

Mississippi

A

Name	City	Address	State	Zip	Telephone
Ascot Surety & Casualty Company	Parker	10233 South Parker Road Suite	CO	80134	414-369-5033

A-

Name	City	Address	State	Zip	Telephone
Cincinnati Indemnity Co	Fairfield	6200 South Gilmore Road	OH	45014	414-369-5033

B+

Name	City	Address	State	Zip	Telephone
USAA General Indemnity Co	San Antonio	9800 Fredericksburg Road	TX	78288	414-369-5033
USAA Casualty Ins Co	San Antonio	9800 Fredericksburg Road	TX	78288	414-369-5033
Travelers Indemnity Co	Hartford	One Tower Square	CT	6183	414-369-5033
Travelers Casualty & Surety Co	Hartford	One Tower Square	CT	6183	414-369-5033
State Farm Mutual Automobile Ins Co	Bloomington	One State Farm Plaza	IL	61710	414-369-5033
State Farm Fire & Cas Co	Bloomington	One State Farm Plaza	IL	61710	414-369-5033
Sentry Ins A Mutual Co	Stevens Point	1800 North Point Drive	WI	54481	414-369-5033
Sentry Casualty Co	Stevens Point	1800 North Point Drive	WI	54481	414-369-5033
Securian Casualty Co	St. Paul	400 Robert Street North	MN	55101	414-369-5033
Geico General Ins Co	Omaha	3555 Farnam Street Suite 1440	NE	68131	414-369-5033
Frankenmuth Mutual Ins Co	Frankenmuth	One Mutual Avenue	MI	48787	414-369-5033
Cincinnati Ins Co	Fairfield	6200 South Gilmore Road	OH	45014	414-369-5033

Missouri

A-

Name	City	Address	State	Zip	Telephone
Cincinnati Indemnity Co	Fairfield	6200 South Gilmore Road	OH	45014	414-369-5033

Missouri (continued)

B+

Name	City	Address	State	Zip	Telephone
USAA General Indemnity Co	San Antonio	9800 Fredericksburg Road	TX	78288	414-369-5033
USAA Casualty Ins Co	San Antonio	9800 Fredericksburg Road	TX	78288	414-369-5033
Travelers Indemnity Co	Hartford	One Tower Square	CT	6183	414-369-5033
Travelers Casualty & Surety Co	Hartford	One Tower Square	CT	6183	414-369-5033
State Farm Mutual Automobile Ins Co	Bloomington	One State Farm Plaza	IL	61710	414-369-5033
State Farm Fire & Cas Co	Bloomington	One State Farm Plaza	IL	61710	414-369-5033
Sentry Ins A Mutual Co	Stevens Point	1800 North Point Drive	WI	54481	414-369-5033
Sentry Casualty Co	Stevens Point	1800 North Point Drive	WI	54481	414-369-5033
Securian Casualty Co	St. Paul	400 Robert Street North	MN	55101	414-369-5033
Owners Ins Co	Lima	2325 North Cole Street	OH	45801	414-369-5033
Home-Owners Ins Co	Lansing	6101 Anacapri Boulevard	MI	48917	414-369-5033
Geico General Ins Co	Omaha	3555 Farnam Street Suite 1440	NE	68131	414-369-5033
Frankenmuth Mutual Ins Co	Frankenmuth	One Mutual Avenue	MI	48787	414-369-5033
Country Mutual Ins Co	Bloomington	1701 Towanda Avenue	IL	61701	414-369-5033
Cincinnati Ins Co	Fairfield	6200 South Gilmore Road	OH	45014	414-369-5033
Auto-Owners Ins Co	Lansing	6101 Anacapri Boulevard	MI	48917	414-369-5033
American Standard Ins Co of WI	Madison	6000 American Parkway	WI	53783	414-369-5033
Acuity A Mutual Ins Co	Sheboygan	2800 South Taylor Drive	WI	53081	414-369-5033

Montana

A

Name	City	Address	State	Zip	Telephone
Ascot Surety & Casualty Company	Parker	10233 South Parker Road Suite	CO	80134	414-369-5033

A-

Name	City	Address	State	Zip	Telephone
Cincinnati Indemnity Co	Fairfield	6200 South Gilmore Road	OH	45014	414-369-5033

B+

Name	City	Address	State	Zip	Telephone
USAA General Indemnity Co	San Antonio	9800 Fredericksburg Road	TX	78288	414-369-5033
USAA Casualty Ins Co	San Antonio	9800 Fredericksburg Road	TX	78288	414-369-5033
Travelers Indemnity Co	Hartford	One Tower Square	CT	6183	414-369-5033
Travelers Casualty & Surety Co	Hartford	One Tower Square	CT	6183	414-369-5033
State Farm Mutual Automobile Ins Co	Bloomington	One State Farm Plaza	IL	61710	414-369-5033

Montana (continued)

B+

Name	City	Address	State	Zip	Telephone
State Farm Fire & Cas Co	Bloomington	One State Farm Plaza	IL	61710	414-369-5033
Sentry Ins A Mutual Co	Stevens Point	1800 North Point Drive	WI	54481	414-369-5033
Sentry Casualty Co	Stevens Point	1800 North Point Drive	WI	54481	414-369-5033
Securian Casualty Co	St. Paul	400 Robert Street North	MN	55101	414-369-5033
Geico General Ins Co	Omaha	3555 Farnam Street Suite 1440	NE	68131	414-369-5033
Country Mutual Ins Co	Bloomington	1701 Towanda Avenue	IL	61701	414-369-5033
Cincinnati Ins Co	Fairfield	6200 South Gilmore Road	OH	45014	414-369-5033
Acuity A Mutual Ins Co	Sheboygan	2800 South Taylor Drive	WI	53081	414-369-5033

Nebraska

A

Name	City	Address	State	Zip	Telephone
Ascot Surety & Casualty Company	Parker	10233 South Parker Road Suite	CO	80134	414-369-5033

A-

Name	City	Address	State	Zip	Telephone
Cincinnati Indemnity Co	Fairfield	6200 South Gilmore Road	OH	45014	414-369-5033

B+

Name	City	Address	State	Zip	Telephone
USAA General Indemnity Co	San Antonio	9800 Fredericksburg Road	TX	78288	414-369-5033
USAA Casualty Ins Co	San Antonio	9800 Fredericksburg Road	TX	78288	414-369-5033
Travelers Indemnity Co	Hartford	One Tower Square	CT	6183	414-369-5033
Travelers Casualty & Surety Co	Hartford	One Tower Square	CT	6183	414-369-5033
State Farm Mutual Automobile Ins Co	Bloomington	One State Farm Plaza	IL	61710	414-369-5033
State Farm Fire & Cas Co	Bloomington	One State Farm Plaza	IL	61710	414-369-5033
Sentry Ins A Mutual Co	Stevens Point	1800 North Point Drive	WI	54481	414-369-5033
Sentry Casualty Co	Stevens Point	1800 North Point Drive	WI	54481	414-369-5033
Securian Casualty Co	St. Paul	400 Robert Street North	MN	55101	414-369-5033
Owners Ins Co	Lima	2325 North Cole Street	OH	45801	414-369-5033
Geico General Ins Co	Omaha	3555 Farnam Street Suite 1440	NE	68131	414-369-5033
Country Mutual Ins Co	Bloomington	1701 Towanda Avenue	IL	61701	414-369-5033
Cincinnati Ins Co	Fairfield	6200 South Gilmore Road	OH	45014	414-369-5033
Auto-Owners Ins Co	Lansing	6101 Anacapri Boulevard	MI	48917	414-369-5033
American Standard Ins Co of WI	Madison	6000 American Parkway	WI	53783	414-369-5033

Nebraska (continued)

B+

Name	City	Address	State	Zip	Telephone
Acuity A Mutual Ins Co	Sheboygan	2800 South Taylor Drive	WI	53081	414-369-5033

Nevada

A

Name	City	Address	State	Zip	Telephone
Ascot Surety & Casualty Company	Parker	10233 South Parker Road Suite	CO	80134	414-369-5033

A-

Name	City	Address	State	Zip	Telephone
Cincinnati Indemnity Co	Fairfield	6200 South Gilmore Road	OH	45014	414-369-5033

B+

Name	City	Address	State	Zip	Telephone
USAA General Indemnity Co	San Antonio	9800 Fredericksburg Road	TX	78288	414-369-5033
USAA Casualty Ins Co	San Antonio	9800 Fredericksburg Road	TX	78288	414-369-5033
Travelers Indemnity Co	Hartford	One Tower Square	CT	6183	414-369-5033
Travelers Casualty & Surety Co	Hartford	One Tower Square	CT	6183	414-369-5033
State Farm Mutual Automobile Ins Co	Bloomington	One State Farm Plaza	IL	61710	414-369-5033
State Farm Fire & Cas Co	Bloomington	One State Farm Plaza	IL	61710	414-369-5033
Sentry Ins A Mutual Co	Stevens Point	1800 North Point Drive	WI	54481	414-369-5033
Sentry Casualty Co	Stevens Point	1800 North Point Drive	WI	54481	414-369-5033
Securian Casualty Co	St. Paul	400 Robert Street North	MN	55101	414-369-5033
Geico General Ins Co	Omaha	3555 Farnam Street Suite 1440	NE	68131	414-369-5033
Country Mutual Ins Co	Bloomington	1701 Towanda Avenue	IL	61701	414-369-5033
Cincinnati Ins Co	Fairfield	6200 South Gilmore Road	OH	45014	414-369-5033
American Standard Ins Co of WI	Madison	6000 American Parkway	WI	53783	414-369-5033
Acuity A Mutual Ins Co	Sheboygan	2800 South Taylor Drive	WI	53081	414-369-5033

New Hampshire

A-

Name	City	Address	State	Zip	Telephone
Cincinnati Indemnity Co	Fairfield	6200 South Gilmore Road	OH	45014	414-369-5033

New Hampshire (continued)

B+

Name	City	Address	State	Zip	Telephone
USAA General Indemnity Co	San Antonio	9800 Fredericksburg Road	TX	78288	414-369-5033
USAA Casualty Ins Co	San Antonio	9800 Fredericksburg Road	TX	78288	414-369-5033
Travelers Indemnity Co	Hartford	One Tower Square	CT	6183	414-369-5033
Travelers Casualty & Surety Co	Hartford	One Tower Square	CT	6183	414-369-5033
State Farm Mutual Automobile Ins Co	Bloomington	One State Farm Plaza	IL	61710	414-369-5033
State Farm Fire & Cas Co	Bloomington	One State Farm Plaza	IL	61710	414-369-5033
Sentry Ins A Mutual Co	Stevens Point	1800 North Point Drive	WI	54481	414-369-5033
Sentry Casualty Co	Stevens Point	1800 North Point Drive	WI	54481	414-369-5033
Securian Casualty Co	St. Paul	400 Robert Street North	MN	55101	414-369-5033
Interins Exchange	Costa Mesa	3333 Fairview Road	CA	92626	414-369-5033
Geico General Ins Co	Omaha	3555 Farnam Street Suite 1440	NE	68131	414-369-5033
Frankenmuth Mutual Ins Co	Frankenmuth	One Mutual Avenue	MI	48787	414-369-5033
Farm Family Casualty Ins Co	Glenmont	344 Route 9w	NY	12077	414-369-5033
Country Mutual Ins Co	Bloomington	1701 Towanda Avenue	IL	61701	414-369-5033
Cincinnati Ins Co	Fairfield	6200 South Gilmore Road	OH	45014	414-369-5033
Acuity A Mutual Ins Co	Sheboygan	2800 South Taylor Drive	WI	53081	414-369-5033

New Jersey

A-

Name	City	Address	State	Zip	Telephone
Selective Casualty Insurance Company	Branchville	40 Wantage Ave	NJ	7890	414-369-5033
Progressive Garden State Ins Co	West Trenton	820 Bear Tavern Rd Suite 305	NJ	08628	414-369-5033
Cincinnati Indemnity Co	Fairfield	6200 South Gilmore Road	OH	45014	414-369-5033

B+

Name	City	Address	State	Zip	Telephone
USAA General Indemnity Co	San Antonio	9800 Fredericksburg Road	TX	78288	414-369-5033
USAA Casualty Ins Co	San Antonio	9800 Fredericksburg Road	TX	78288	414-369-5033
Travelers Indemnity Co	Hartford	One Tower Square	CT	6183	414-369-5033
Travelers Casualty & Surety Co	Hartford	One Tower Square	CT	6183	414-369-5033
State Farm Mutual Automobile Ins Co	Bloomington	One State Farm Plaza	IL	61710	414-369-5033
State Farm Fire & Cas Co	Bloomington	One State Farm Plaza	IL	61710	414-369-5033
Sentry Ins A Mutual Co	Stevens Point	1800 North Point Drive	WI	54481	414-369-5033
Sentry Casualty Co	Stevens Point	1800 North Point Drive	WI	54481	414-369-5033
Selective Fire and Casualty Insurance	Branchville	40 Wantage Ave	NJ	7890	414-369-5033

New Jersey (continued)

B+

Name	City	Address	State	Zip	Telephone
Securian Casualty Co	St. Paul	400 Robert Street North	MN	55101	414-369-5033
Frankenmuth Mutual Ins Co	Frankenmuth	One Mutual Avenue	MI	48787	414-369-5033
Farm Family Casualty Ins Co	Glenmont	344 Route 9w	NY	12077	414-369-5033
Country Mutual Ins Co	Bloomington	1701 Towanda Avenue	IL	61701	414-369-5033
Cincinnati Ins Co	Fairfield	6200 South Gilmore Road	OH	45014	414-369-5033

New Mexico

A-

Name	City	Address	State	Zip	Telephone
Cincinnati Indemnity Co	Fairfield	6200 South Gilmore Road	OH	45014	414-369-5033

B+

Name	City	Address	State	Zip	Telephone
USAA General Indemnity Co	San Antonio	9800 Fredericksburg Road	TX	78288	414-369-5033
USAA Casualty Ins Co	San Antonio	9800 Fredericksburg Road	TX	78288	414-369-5033
Travelers Indemnity Co	Hartford	One Tower Square	CT	6183	414-369-5033
Travelers Casualty & Surety Co	Hartford	One Tower Square	CT	6183	414-369-5033
State Farm Mutual Automobile Ins Co	Bloomington	One State Farm Plaza	IL	61710	414-369-5033
State Farm Fire & Cas Co	Bloomington	One State Farm Plaza	IL	61710	414-369-5033
Sentry Ins A Mutual Co	Stevens Point	1800 North Point Drive	WI	54481	414-369-5033
Sentry Casualty Co	Stevens Point	1800 North Point Drive	WI	54481	414-369-5033
Securian Casualty Co	St. Paul	400 Robert Street North	MN	55101	414-369-5033
Interins Exchange	Costa Mesa	3333 Fairview Road	CA	92626	414-369-5033
Geico General Ins Co	Omaha	3555 Farnam Street Suite 1440	NE	68131	414-369-5033
Cincinnati Ins Co	Fairfield	6200 South Gilmore Road	OH	45014	414-369-5033
Acuity A Mutual Ins Co	Sheboygan	2800 South Taylor Drive	WI	53081	414-369-5033

New York

A-

Name	City	Address	State	Zip	Telephone
Cincinnati Indemnity Co	Fairfield	6200 South Gilmore Road	OH	45014	414-369-5033
Aca Financial Guaranty Corp	Baltimore	7 Saint Paul Street Suite 1660	MD	21202	414-369-5033

New York (continued)

B+

Name	City	Address	State	Zip	Telephone
USAA General Indemnity Co	San Antonio	9800 Fredericksburg Road	TX	78288	414-369-5033
USAA Casualty Ins Co	San Antonio	9800 Fredericksburg Road	TX	78288	414-369-5033
Travelers Indemnity Co	Hartford	One Tower Square	CT	6183	414-369-5033
Travelers Casualty & Surety Co	Hartford	One Tower Square	CT	6183	414-369-5033
State Farm Mutual Automobile Ins Co	Bloomington	One State Farm Plaza	IL	61710	414-369-5033
State Farm Fire & Cas Co	Bloomington	One State Farm Plaza	IL	61710	414-369-5033
Sentry Ins A Mutual Co	Stevens Point	1800 North Point Drive	WI	54481	414-369-5033
Sentry Casualty Co	Stevens Point	1800 North Point Drive	WI	54481	414-369-5033
Securian Casualty Co	St. Paul	400 Robert Street North	MN	55101	414-369-5033
Geico General Ins Co	Omaha	3555 Farnam Street Suite 1440	NE	68131	414-369-5033
Frankenmuth Mutual Ins Co	Frankenmuth	One Mutual Avenue	MI	48787	414-369-5033
Farm Family Casualty Ins Co	Glenmont	344 Route 9w	NY	12077	414-369-5033
Country Mutual Ins Co	Bloomington	1701 Towanda Avenue	IL	61701	414-369-5033
Cincinnati Ins Co	Fairfield	6200 South Gilmore Road	OH	45014	414-369-5033

North Carolina

A

Name	City	Address	State	Zip	Telephone
Ascot Surety & Casualty Company	Parker	10233 South Parker Road Suite	CO	80134	414-369-5033

A-

Name	City	Address	State	Zip	Telephone
Cincinnati Indemnity Co	Fairfield	6200 South Gilmore Road	OH	45014	414-369-5033

B+

Name	City	Address	State	Zip	Telephone
USAA General Indemnity Co	San Antonio	9800 Fredericksburg Road	TX	78288	414-369-5033
USAA Casualty Ins Co	San Antonio	9800 Fredericksburg Road	TX	78288	414-369-5033
Travelers Indemnity Co	Hartford	One Tower Square	CT	6183	414-369-5033
Travelers Casualty & Surety Co	Hartford	One Tower Square	CT	6183	414-369-5033
State Farm Mutual Automobile Ins Co	Bloomington	One State Farm Plaza	IL	61710	414-369-5033
State Farm Fire & Cas Co	Bloomington	One State Farm Plaza	IL	61710	414-369-5033
Sentry Ins A Mutual Co	Stevens Point	1800 North Point Drive	WI	54481	414-369-5033
Sentry Casualty Co	Stevens Point	1800 North Point Drive	WI	54481	414-369-5033
Securian Casualty Co	St. Paul	400 Robert Street North	MN	55101	414-369-5033

North Carolina (continued)

B+

Name	City	Address	State	Zip	Telephone
Owners Ins Co	Lima	2325 North Cole Street	OH	45801	414-369-5033
Frankenmuth Mutual Ins Co	Frankenmuth	One Mutual Avenue	MI	48787	414-369-5033
Country Mutual Ins Co	Bloomington	1701 Towanda Avenue	IL	61701	414-369-5033
Cincinnati Ins Co	Fairfield	6200 South Gilmore Road	OH	45014	414-369-5033
Auto-Owners Ins Co	Lansing	6101 Anacapri Boulevard	MI	48917	414-369-5033
Alfa Alliance Ins Corp	Montgomery	4480 Cox Road Suite 300	AL	36116	414-369-5033

North Dakota

A

Name	City	Address	State	Zip	Telephone
Ascot Surety & Casualty Company	Parker	10233 South Parker Road Suite	CO	80134	414-369-5033

A-

Name	City	Address	State	Zip	Telephone
Cincinnati Indemnity Co	Fairfield	6200 South Gilmore Road	OH	45014	414-369-5033

B+

Name	City	Address	State	Zip	Telephone
USAA General Indemnity Co	San Antonio	9800 Fredericksburg Road	TX	78288	414-369-5033
USAA Casualty Ins Co	San Antonio	9800 Fredericksburg Road	TX	78288	414-369-5033
Travelers Indemnity Co	Hartford	One Tower Square	CT	6183	414-369-5033
Travelers Casualty & Surety Co	Hartford	One Tower Square	CT	6183	414-369-5033
State Farm Mutual Automobile Ins Co	Bloomington	One State Farm Plaza	IL	61710	414-369-5033
State Farm Fire & Cas Co	Bloomington	One State Farm Plaza	IL	61710	414-369-5033
Sentry Ins A Mutual Co	Stevens Point	1800 North Point Drive	WI	54481	414-369-5033
Sentry Casualty Co	Stevens Point	1800 North Point Drive	WI	54481	414-369-5033
Securian Casualty Co	St. Paul	400 Robert Street North	MN	55101	414-369-5033
Owners Ins Co	Lima	2325 North Cole Street	OH	45801	414-369-5033
Geico General Ins Co	Omaha	3555 Farnam Street Suite 1440	NE	68131	414-369-5033
Frankenmuth Mutual Ins Co	Frankenmuth	One Mutual Avenue	MI	48787	414-369-5033
Country Mutual Ins Co	Bloomington	1701 Towanda Avenue	IL	61701	414-369-5033
Cincinnati Ins Co	Fairfield	6200 South Gilmore Road	OH	45014	414-369-5033
Auto-Owners Ins Co	Lansing	6101 Anacapri Boulevard	MI	48917	414-369-5033
American Standard Ins Co of WI	Madison	6000 American Parkway	WI	53783	414-369-5033
Acuity A Mutual Ins Co	Sheboygan	2800 South Taylor Drive	WI	53081	414-369-5033

Ohio

A-

Name	City	Address	State	Zip	Telephone
Cincinnati Indemnity Co	Fairfield	6200 South Gilmore Road	OH	45014	414-369-5033

B+

Name	City	Address	State	Zip	Telephone
USAA General Indemnity Co	San Antonio	9800 Fredericksburg Road	TX	78288	414-369-5033
USAA Casualty Ins Co	San Antonio	9800 Fredericksburg Road	TX	78288	414-369-5033
Travelers Indemnity Co	Hartford	One Tower Square	CT	6183	414-369-5033
Travelers Casualty & Surety Co	Hartford	One Tower Square	CT	6183	414-369-5033
State Farm Mutual Automobile Ins Co	Bloomington	One State Farm Plaza	IL	61710	414-369-5033
State Farm Fire & Cas Co	Bloomington	One State Farm Plaza	IL	61710	414-369-5033
Sentry Ins A Mutual Co	Stevens Point	1800 North Point Drive	WI	54481	414-369-5033
Sentry Casualty Co	Stevens Point	1800 North Point Drive	WI	54481	414-369-5033
Securian Casualty Co	St. Paul	400 Robert Street North	MN	55101	414-369-5033
Owners Ins Co	Lima	2325 North Cole Street	OH	45801	414-369-5033
Motorists Mutual Ins Co	Columbus	471 East Broad Street	OH	43215	414-369-5033
Home-Owners Ins Co	Lansing	6101 Anacapri Boulevard	MI	48917	414-369-5033
Geico General Ins Co	Omaha	3555 Farnam Street Suite 1440	NE	68131	414-369-5033
Frankenmuth Mutual Ins Co	Frankenmuth	One Mutual Avenue	MI	48787	414-369-5033
Country Mutual Ins Co	Bloomington	1701 Towanda Avenue	IL	61701	414-369-5033
Cincinnati Ins Co	Fairfield	6200 South Gilmore Road	OH	45014	414-369-5033
Auto-Owners Ins Co	Lansing	6101 Anacapri Boulevard	MI	48917	414-369-5033
American Standard Ins Co of WI	Madison	6000 American Parkway	WI	53783	414-369-5033
Acuity A Mutual Ins Co	Sheboygan	2800 South Taylor Drive	WI	53081	414-369-5033

Oklahoma

A-

Name	City	Address	State	Zip	Telephone
Cincinnati Indemnity Co	Fairfield	6200 South Gilmore Road	OH	45014	414-369-5033

B+

Name	City	Address	State	Zip	Telephone
USAA General Indemnity Co	San Antonio	9800 Fredericksburg Road	TX	78288	414-369-5033
USAA Casualty Ins Co	San Antonio	9800 Fredericksburg Road	TX	78288	414-369-5033
Travelers Indemnity Co	Hartford	One Tower Square	CT	6183	414-369-5033
Travelers Casualty & Surety Co	Hartford	One Tower Square	CT	6183	414-369-5033

Oklahoma (continued)

B+

Name	City	Address	State	Zip	Telephone
State Farm Mutual Automobile Ins Co	Bloomington	One State Farm Plaza	IL	61710	414-369-5033
State Farm Fire & Cas Co	Bloomington	One State Farm Plaza	IL	61710	414-369-5033
Sentry Ins A Mutual Co	Stevens Point	1800 North Point Drive	WI	54481	414-369-5033
Sentry Casualty Co	Stevens Point	1800 North Point Drive	WI	54481	414-369-5033
Securian Casualty Co	St. Paul	400 Robert Street North	MN	55101	414-369-5033
Geico General Ins Co	Omaha	3555 Farnam Street Suite 1440	NE	68131	414-369-5033
Country Mutual Ins Co	Bloomington	1701 Towanda Avenue	IL	61701	414-369-5033
Cincinnati Ins Co	Fairfield	6200 South Gilmore Road	OH	45014	414-369-5033

Oregon

A-

Name	City	Address	State	Zip	Telephone
Cincinnati Indemnity Co	Fairfield	6200 South Gilmore Road	OH	45014	414-369-5033

B+

Name	City	Address	State	Zip	Telephone
USAA General Indemnity Co	San Antonio	9800 Fredericksburg Road	TX	78288	414-369-5033
USAA Casualty Ins Co	San Antonio	9800 Fredericksburg Road	TX	78288	414-369-5033
Travelers Indemnity Co	Hartford	One Tower Square	CT	6183	414-369-5033
Travelers Casualty & Surety Co	Hartford	One Tower Square	CT	6183	414-369-5033
State Farm Mutual Automobile Ins Co	Bloomington	One State Farm Plaza	IL	61710	414-369-5033
State Farm Fire & Cas Co	Bloomington	One State Farm Plaza	IL	61710	414-369-5033
Sentry Ins A Mutual Co	Stevens Point	1800 North Point Drive	WI	54481	414-369-5033
Sentry Casualty Co	Stevens Point	1800 North Point Drive	WI	54481	414-369-5033
Securian Casualty Co	St. Paul	400 Robert Street North	MN	55101	414-369-5033
Geico General Ins Co	Omaha	3555 Farnam Street Suite 1440	NE	68131	414-369-5033
Country Mutual Ins Co	Bloomington	1701 Towanda Avenue	IL	61701	414-369-5033
Cincinnati Ins Co	Fairfield	6200 South Gilmore Road	OH	45014	414-369-5033
American Standard Ins Co of WI	Madison	6000 American Parkway	WI	53783	414-369-5033

Pennsylvania

A

Name	City	Address	State	Zip	Telephone
Ascot Surety & Casualty Company	Parker	10233 South Parker Road Suite	CO	80134	414-369-5033

Pennsylvania (continued)

A-

Name	City	Address	State	Zip	Telephone
Cincinnati Indemnity Co	Fairfield	6200 South Gilmore Road	OH	45014	414-369-5033
Aca Financial Guaranty Corp	Baltimore	7 Saint Paul Street Suite 1660	MD	21202	414-369-5033

B+

Name	City	Address	State	Zip	Telephone
Westguard Ins Co	Wilkes-Barre	39 Public Square	PA	18701	414-369-5033
USAA General Indemnity Co	San Antonio	9800 Fredericksburg Road	TX	78288	414-369-5033
USAA Casualty Ins Co	San Antonio	9800 Fredericksburg Road	TX	78288	414-369-5033
Travelers Indemnity Co	Hartford	One Tower Square	CT	6183	414-369-5033
Travelers Casualty & Surety Co	Hartford	One Tower Square	CT	6183	414-369-5033
State Farm Mutual Automobile Ins Co	Bloomington	One State Farm Plaza	IL	61710	414-369-5033
State Farm Fire & Cas Co	Bloomington	One State Farm Plaza	IL	61710	414-369-5033
Sentry Ins A Mutual Co	Stevens Point	1800 North Point Drive	WI	54481	414-369-5033
Sentry Casualty Co	Stevens Point	1800 North Point Drive	WI	54481	414-369-5033
Securian Casualty Co	St. Paul	400 Robert Street North	MN	55101	414-369-5033
Owners Ins Co	Lima	2325 North Cole Street	OH	45801	414-369-5033
Motorists Mutual Ins Co	Columbus	471 East Broad Street	OH	43215	414-369-5033
Interins Exchange	Costa Mesa	3333 Fairview Road	CA	92626	414-369-5033
Geico General Ins Co	Omaha	3555 Farnam Street Suite 1440	NE	68131	414-369-5033
Frankenmuth Mutual Ins Co	Frankenmuth	One Mutual Avenue	MI	48787	414-369-5033
Farm Family Casualty Ins Co	Glenmont	344 Route 9w	NY	12077	414-369-5033
Country Mutual Ins Co	Bloomington	1701 Towanda Avenue	IL	61701	414-369-5033
Cincinnati Ins Co	Fairfield	6200 South Gilmore Road	OH	45014	414-369-5033
Auto-Owners Ins Co	Lansing	6101 Anacapri Boulevard	MI	48917	414-369-5033
Acuity A Mutual Ins Co	Sheboygan	2800 South Taylor Drive	WI	53081	414-369-5033

Rhode Island

A-

Name	City	Address	State	Zip	Telephone
Cincinnati Indemnity Co	Fairfield	6200 South Gilmore Road	OH	45014	414-369-5033

B+

Name	City	Address	State	Zip	Telephone
USAA General Indemnity Co	San Antonio	9800 Fredericksburg Road	TX	78288	414-369-5033
USAA Casualty Ins Co	San Antonio	9800 Fredericksburg Road	TX	78288	414-369-5033

Rhode Island (continued)

B+

Name	City	Address	State	Zip	Telephone
Travelers Indemnity Co	Hartford	One Tower Square	CT	6183	414-369-5033
Travelers Casualty & Surety Co	Hartford	One Tower Square	CT	6183	414-369-5033
State Farm Mutual Automobile Ins Co	Bloomington	One State Farm Plaza	IL	61710	414-369-5033
State Farm Fire & Cas Co	Bloomington	One State Farm Plaza	IL	61710	414-369-5033
Sentry Ins A Mutual Co	Stevens Point	1800 North Point Drive	WI	54481	414-369-5033
Sentry Casualty Co	Stevens Point	1800 North Point Drive	WI	54481	414-369-5033
Securian Casualty Co	St. Paul	400 Robert Street North	MN	55101	414-369-5033
Geico General Ins Co	Omaha	3555 Farnam Street Suite 1440	NE	68131	414-369-5033
Frankenmuth Mutual Ins Co	Frankenmuth	One Mutual Avenue	MI	48787	414-369-5033
Farm Family Casualty Ins Co	Glenmont	344 Route 9w	NY	12077	414-369-5033
Country Mutual Ins Co	Bloomington	1701 Towanda Avenue	IL	61701	414-369-5033
Cincinnati Ins Co	Fairfield	6200 South Gilmore Road	OH	45014	414-369-5033

South Carolina

A-

Name	City	Address	State	Zip	Telephone
Cincinnati Indemnity Co	Fairfield	6200 South Gilmore Road	OH	45014	414-369-5033
Aca Financial Guaranty Corp	Baltimore	7 Saint Paul Street Suite 1660	MD	21202	414-369-5033

B+

Name	City	Address	State	Zip	Telephone
USAA General Indemnity Co	San Antonio	9800 Fredericksburg Road	TX	78288	414-369-5033
USAA Casualty Ins Co	San Antonio	9800 Fredericksburg Road	TX	78288	414-369-5033
Travelers Indemnity Co	Hartford	One Tower Square	CT	6183	414-369-5033
Travelers Casualty & Surety Co	Hartford	One Tower Square	CT	6183	414-369-5033
State Farm Mutual Automobile Ins Co	Bloomington	One State Farm Plaza	IL	61710	414-369-5033
State Farm Fire & Cas Co	Bloomington	One State Farm Plaza	IL	61710	414-369-5033
Sentry Ins A Mutual Co	Stevens Point	1800 North Point Drive	WI	54481	414-369-5033
Sentry Casualty Co	Stevens Point	1800 North Point Drive	WI	54481	414-369-5033
Securian Casualty Co	St. Paul	400 Robert Street North	MN	55101	414-369-5033
Owners Ins Co	Lima	2325 North Cole Street	OH	45801	414-369-5033
Frankenmuth Mutual Ins Co	Frankenmuth	One Mutual Avenue	MI	48787	414-369-5033
Country Mutual Ins Co	Bloomington	1701 Towanda Avenue	IL	61701	414-369-5033
Cincinnati Ins Co	Fairfield	6200 South Gilmore Road	OH	45014	414-369-5033
Auto-Owners Ins Co	Lansing	6101 Anacapri Boulevard	MI	48917	414-369-5033

South Dakota

A

Name	City	Address	State	Zip	Telephone
Ascot Surety & Casualty Company	Parker	10233 South Parker Road Suite	CO	80134	414-369-5033

A-

Name	City	Address	State	Zip	Telephone
Cincinnati Indemnity Co	Fairfield	6200 South Gilmore Road	OH	45014	414-369-5033

B+

Name	City	Address	State	Zip	Telephone
USAA General Indemnity Co	San Antonio	9800 Fredericksburg Road	TX	78288	414-369-5033
USAA Casualty Ins Co	San Antonio	9800 Fredericksburg Road	TX	78288	414-369-5033
Travelers Indemnity Co	Hartford	One Tower Square	CT	6183	414-369-5033
Travelers Casualty & Surety Co	Hartford	One Tower Square	CT	6183	414-369-5033
State Farm Mutual Automobile Ins Co	Bloomington	One State Farm Plaza	IL	61710	414-369-5033
State Farm Fire & Cas Co	Bloomington	One State Farm Plaza	IL	61710	414-369-5033
Sentry Ins A Mutual Co	Stevens Point	1800 North Point Drive	WI	54481	414-369-5033
Sentry Casualty Co	Stevens Point	1800 North Point Drive	WI	54481	414-369-5033
Securian Casualty Co	St. Paul	400 Robert Street North	MN	55101	414-369-5033
Owners Ins Co	Lima	2325 North Cole Street	OH	45801	414-369-5033
Home-Owners Ins Co	Lansing	6101 Anacapri Boulevard	MI	48917	414-369-5033
Geico General Ins Co	Omaha	3555 Farnam Street Suite 1440	NE	68131	414-369-5033
Country Mutual Ins Co	Bloomington	1701 Towanda Avenue	IL	61701	414-369-5033
Cincinnati Ins Co	Fairfield	6200 South Gilmore Road	OH	45014	414-369-5033
Auto-Owners Ins Co	Lansing	6101 Anacapri Boulevard	MI	48917	414-369-5033
American Standard Ins Co of WI	Madison	6000 American Parkway	WI	53783	414-369-5033
Acuity A Mutual Ins Co	Sheboygan	2800 South Taylor Drive	WI	53081	414-369-5033

Tennessee

A

Name	City	Address	State	Zip	Telephone
Ascot Surety & Casualty Company	Parker	10233 South Parker Road Suite	CO	80134	414-369-5033

A-

Name	City	Address	State	Zip	Telephone
Cincinnati Indemnity Co	Fairfield	6200 South Gilmore Road	OH	45014	414-369-5033

Tennessee (continued)

B+

Name	City	Address	State	Zip	Telephone
USAA General Indemnity Co	San Antonio	9800 Fredericksburg Road	TX	78288	414-369-5033
USAA Casualty Ins Co	San Antonio	9800 Fredericksburg Road	TX	78288	414-369-5033
Travelers Indemnity Co	Hartford	One Tower Square	CT	6183	414-369-5033
Travelers Casualty & Surety Co	Hartford	One Tower Square	CT	6183	414-369-5033
Tennessee Farmers Mutual Ins Co	Columbia	147 Bear Creek Pike	TN	38401	414-369-5033
State Farm Mutual Automobile Ins Co	Bloomington	One State Farm Plaza	IL	61710	414-369-5033
State Farm Fire & Cas Co	Bloomington	One State Farm Plaza	IL	61710	414-369-5033
Sentry Ins A Mutual Co	Stevens Point	1800 North Point Drive	WI	54481	414-369-5033
Sentry Casualty Co	Stevens Point	1800 North Point Drive	WI	54481	414-369-5033
Securian Casualty Co	St. Paul	400 Robert Street North	MN	55101	414-369-5033
Owners Ins Co	Lima	2325 North Cole Street	OH	45801	414-369-5033
Geico General Ins Co	Omaha	3555 Farnam Street Suite 1440	NE	68131	414-369-5033
Frankenmuth Mutual Ins Co	Frankenmuth	One Mutual Avenue	MI	48787	414-369-5033
Country Mutual Ins Co	Bloomington	1701 Towanda Avenue	IL	61701	414-369-5033
Cincinnati Ins Co	Fairfield	6200 South Gilmore Road	OH	45014	414-369-5033
Auto-Owners Ins Co	Lansing	6101 Anacapri Boulevard	MI	48917	414-369-5033
Acuity A Mutual Ins Co	Sheboygan	2800 South Taylor Drive	WI	53081	414-369-5033

Texas

A-

Name	City	Address	State	Zip	Telephone
Cincinnati Indemnity Co	Fairfield	6200 South Gilmore Road	OH	45014	414-369-5033
Aca Financial Guaranty Corp	Baltimore	7 Saint Paul Street Suite 1660	MD	21202	414-369-5033

B+

Name	City	Address	State	Zip	Telephone
USAA General Indemnity Co	San Antonio	9800 Fredericksburg Road	TX	78288	414-369-5033
USAA Casualty Ins Co	San Antonio	9800 Fredericksburg Road	TX	78288	414-369-5033
Travelers Indemnity Co	Hartford	One Tower Square	CT	6183	414-369-5033
Travelers Casualty & Surety Co	Hartford	One Tower Square	CT	6183	414-369-5033
State Farm Mutual Automobile Ins Co	Bloomington	One State Farm Plaza	IL	61710	414-369-5033
State Farm Fire & Cas Co	Bloomington	One State Farm Plaza	IL	61710	414-369-5033
Sentry Ins A Mutual Co	Stevens Point	1800 North Point Drive	WI	54481	414-369-5033
Sentry Casualty Co	Stevens Point	1800 North Point Drive	WI	54481	414-369-5033
Securian Casualty Co	St. Paul	400 Robert Street North	MN	55101	414-369-5033

Texas (continued)

B+

Name	City	Address	State	Zip	Telephone
Interins Exchange	Costa Mesa	3333 Fairview Road	CA	92626	414-369-5033
Geico General Ins Co	Omaha	3555 Farnam Street Suite 1440	NE	68131	414-369-5033
Frankenmuth Mutual Ins Co	Frankenmuth	One Mutual Avenue	MI	48787	414-369-5033
Cincinnati Ins Co	Fairfield	6200 South Gilmore Road	OH	45014	414-369-5033
Acuity A Mutual Ins Co	Sheboygan	2800 South Taylor Drive	WI	53081	414-369-5033

Utah

A-

Name	City	Address	State	Zip	Telephone
Cincinnati Indemnity Co	Fairfield	6200 South Gilmore Road	OH	45014	414-369-5033

B+

Name	City	Address	State	Zip	Telephone
USAA General Indemnity Co	San Antonio	9800 Fredericksburg Road	TX	78288	414-369-5033
USAA Casualty Ins Co	San Antonio	9800 Fredericksburg Road	TX	78288	414-369-5033
Travelers Indemnity Co	Hartford	One Tower Square	CT	6183	414-369-5033
Travelers Casualty & Surety Co	Hartford	One Tower Square	CT	6183	414-369-5033
State Farm Mutual Automobile Ins Co	Bloomington	One State Farm Plaza	IL	61710	414-369-5033
State Farm Fire & Cas Co	Bloomington	One State Farm Plaza	IL	61710	414-369-5033
Sentry Ins A Mutual Co	Stevens Point	1800 North Point Drive	WI	54481	414-369-5033
Sentry Casualty Co	Stevens Point	1800 North Point Drive	WI	54481	414-369-5033
Securian Casualty Co	St. Paul	400 Robert Street North	MN	55101	414-369-5033
Owners Ins Co	Lima	2325 North Cole Street	OH	45801	414-369-5033
Home-Owners Ins Co	Lansing	6101 Anacapri Boulevard	MI	48917	414-369-5033
Geico General Ins Co	Omaha	3555 Farnam Street Suite 1440	NE	68131	414-369-5033
Country Mutual Ins Co	Bloomington	1701 Towanda Avenue	IL	61701	414-369-5033
Cincinnati Ins Co	Fairfield	6200 South Gilmore Road	OH	45014	414-369-5033
Auto-Owners Ins Co	Lansing	6101 Anacapri Boulevard	MI	48917	414-369-5033
American Standard Ins Co of WI	Madison	6000 American Parkway	WI	53783	414-369-5033
Acuity A Mutual Ins Co	Sheboygan	2800 South Taylor Drive	WI	53081	414-369-5033

Vermont

A-

Name	City	Address	State	Zip	Telephone
Cincinnati Indemnity Co	Fairfield	6200 South Gilmore Road	OH	45014	414-369-5033
Aca Financial Guaranty Corp	Baltimore	7 Saint Paul Street Suite 1660	MD	21202	414-369-5033

B+

Name	City	Address	State	Zip	Telephone
USAA General Indemnity Co	San Antonio	9800 Fredericksburg Road	TX	78288	414-369-5033
USAA Casualty Ins Co	San Antonio	9800 Fredericksburg Road	TX	78288	414-369-5033
Travelers Indemnity Co	Hartford	One Tower Square	CT	6183	414-369-5033
Travelers Casualty & Surety Co	Hartford	One Tower Square	CT	6183	414-369-5033
State Farm Mutual Automobile Ins Co	Bloomington	One State Farm Plaza	IL	61710	414-369-5033
State Farm Fire & Cas Co	Bloomington	One State Farm Plaza	IL	61710	414-369-5033
Sentry Ins A Mutual Co	Stevens Point	1800 North Point Drive	WI	54481	414-369-5033
Sentry Casualty Co	Stevens Point	1800 North Point Drive	WI	54481	414-369-5033
Securian Casualty Co	St. Paul	400 Robert Street North	MN	55101	414-369-5033
Interins Exchange	Costa Mesa	3333 Fairview Road	CA	92626	414-369-5033
Geico General Ins Co	Omaha	3555 Farnam Street Suite 1440	NE	68131	414-369-5033
Frankenmuth Mutual Ins Co	Frankenmuth	One Mutual Avenue	MI	48787	414-369-5033
Farm Family Casualty Ins Co	Glenmont	344 Route 9w	NY	12077	414-369-5033
Country Mutual Ins Co	Bloomington	1701 Towanda Avenue	IL	61701	414-369-5033
Cincinnati Ins Co	Fairfield	6200 South Gilmore Road	OH	45014	414-369-5033
Acuity A Mutual Ins Co	Sheboygan	2800 South Taylor Drive	WI	53081	414-369-5033

Virginia

A-

Name	City	Address	State	Zip	Telephone
Cincinnati Indemnity Co	Fairfield	6200 South Gilmore Road	OH	45014	414-369-5033

B+

Name	City	Address	State	Zip	Telephone
USAA General Indemnity Co	San Antonio	9800 Fredericksburg Road	TX	78288	414-369-5033
USAA Casualty Ins Co	San Antonio	9800 Fredericksburg Road	TX	78288	414-369-5033
Travelers Indemnity Co	Hartford	One Tower Square	CT	6183	414-369-5033
Travelers Casualty & Surety Co	Hartford	One Tower Square	CT	6183	414-369-5033
State Farm Mutual Automobile Ins Co	Bloomington	One State Farm Plaza	IL	61710	414-369-5033
State Farm Fire & Cas Co	Bloomington	One State Farm Plaza	IL	61710	414-369-5033

Virginia (continued)

B+

Name	City	Address	State	Zip	Telephone
Sentry Ins A Mutual Co	Stevens Point	1800 North Point Drive	WI	54481	414-369-5033
Sentry Casualty Co	Stevens Point	1800 North Point Drive	WI	54481	414-369-5033
Securian Casualty Co	St. Paul	400 Robert Street North	MN	55101	414-369-5033
Owners Ins Co	Lima	2325 North Cole Street	OH	45801	414-369-5033
Interins Exchange	Costa Mesa	3333 Fairview Road	CA	92626	414-369-5033
Home-Owners Ins Co	Lansing	6101 Anacapri Boulevard	MI	48917	414-369-5033
Geico General Ins Co	Omaha	3555 Farnam Street Suite 1440	NE	68131	414-369-5033
Frankenmuth Mutual Ins Co	Frankenmuth	One Mutual Avenue	MI	48787	414-369-5033
Farm Family Casualty Ins Co	Glenmont	344 Route 9w	NY	12077	414-369-5033
Country Mutual Ins Co	Bloomington	1701 Towanda Avenue	IL	61701	414-369-5033
Cincinnati Ins Co	Fairfield	6200 South Gilmore Road	OH	45014	414-369-5033
Auto-Owners Ins Co	Lansing	6101 Anacapri Boulevard	MI	48917	414-369-5033
Alfa Alliance Ins Corp	Montgomery	4480 Cox Road Suite 300	AL	36116	414-369-5033

Washington

A-

Name	City	Address	State	Zip	Telephone
Cincinnati Indemnity Co	Fairfield	6200 South Gilmore Road	OH	45014	414-369-5033

B+

Name	City	Address	State	Zip	Telephone
USAA General Indemnity Co	San Antonio	9800 Fredericksburg Road	TX	78288	414-369-5033
USAA Casualty Ins Co	San Antonio	9800 Fredericksburg Road	TX	78288	414-369-5033
Travelers Indemnity Co	Hartford	One Tower Square	CT	6183	414-369-5033
Travelers Casualty & Surety Co	Hartford	One Tower Square	CT	6183	414-369-5033
State Farm Mutual Automobile Ins Co	Bloomington	One State Farm Plaza	IL	61710	414-369-5033
State Farm Fire & Cas Co	Bloomington	One State Farm Plaza	IL	61710	414-369-5033
Sentry Ins A Mutual Co	Stevens Point	1800 North Point Drive	WI	54481	414-369-5033
Sentry Casualty Co	Stevens Point	1800 North Point Drive	WI	54481	414-369-5033
Securian Casualty Co	St. Paul	400 Robert Street North	MN	55101	414-369-5033
Geico General Ins Co	Omaha	3555 Farnam Street Suite 1440	NE	68131	414-369-5033
Frankenmuth Mutual Ins Co	Frankenmuth	One Mutual Avenue	MI	48787	414-369-5033
Country Mutual Ins Co	Bloomington	1701 Towanda Avenue	IL	61701	414-369-5033
Cincinnati Ins Co	Fairfield	6200 South Gilmore Road	OH	45014	414-369-5033
American Standard Ins Co of WI	Madison	6000 American Parkway	WI	53783	414-369-5033

West Virginia

A

Name	City	Address	State	Zip	Telephone
Ascot Surety & Casualty Company	Parker	10233 South Parker Road Suite	CO	80134	414-369-5033

A-

Name	City	Address	State	Zip	Telephone
Cincinnati Indemnity Co	Fairfield	6200 South Gilmore Road	OH	45014	414-369-5033

B+

Name	City	Address	State	Zip	Telephone
USAA General Indemnity Co	San Antonio	9800 Fredericksburg Road	TX	78288	414-369-5033
USAA Casualty Ins Co	San Antonio	9800 Fredericksburg Road	TX	78288	414-369-5033
Travelers Indemnity Co	Hartford	One Tower Square	CT	6183	414-369-5033
Travelers Casualty & Surety Co	Hartford	One Tower Square	CT	6183	414-369-5033
State Farm Mutual Automobile Ins Co	Bloomington	One State Farm Plaza	IL	61710	414-369-5033
State Farm Fire & Cas Co	Bloomington	One State Farm Plaza	IL	61710	414-369-5033
Sentry Ins A Mutual Co	Stevens Point	1800 North Point Drive	WI	54481	414-369-5033
Sentry Casualty Co	Stevens Point	1800 North Point Drive	WI	54481	414-369-5033
Securian Casualty Co	St. Paul	400 Robert Street North	MN	55101	414-369-5033
Motorists Mutual Ins Co	Columbus	471 East Broad Street	OH	43215	414-369-5033
Geico General Ins Co	Omaha	3555 Farnam Street Suite 1440	NE	68131	414-369-5033
Frankenmuth Mutual Ins Co	Frankenmuth	One Mutual Avenue	MI	48787	414-369-5033
Farm Family Casualty Ins Co	Glenmont	344 Route 9w	NY	12077	414-369-5033
Cincinnati Ins Co	Fairfield	6200 South Gilmore Road	OH	45014	414-369-5033

Wisconsin

A-

Name	City	Address	State	Zip	Telephone
Cincinnati Indemnity Co	Fairfield	6200 South Gilmore Road	OH	45014	414-369-5033

B+

Name	City	Address	State	Zip	Telephone
USAA General Indemnity Co	San Antonio	9800 Fredericksburg Road	TX	78288	414-369-5033
USAA Casualty Ins Co	San Antonio	9800 Fredericksburg Road	TX	78288	414-369-5033
Travelers Indemnity Co	Hartford	One Tower Square	CT	6183	414-369-5033
Travelers Casualty & Surety Co	Hartford	One Tower Square	CT	6183	414-369-5033
State Farm Mutual Automobile Ins Co	Bloomington	One State Farm Plaza	IL	61710	414-369-5033
State Farm Fire & Cas Co	Bloomington	One State Farm Plaza	IL	61710	414-369-5033

Wisconsin (continued)

B+

Name	City	Address	State	Zip	Telephone
Sentry Ins A Mutual Co	Stevens Point	1800 North Point Drive	WI	54481	414-369-5033
Sentry Casualty Co	Stevens Point	1800 North Point Drive	WI	54481	414-369-5033
Securian Casualty Co	St. Paul	400 Robert Street North	MN	55101	414-369-5033
Owners Ins Co	Lima	2325 North Cole Street	OH	45801	414-369-5033
Geico General Ins Co	Omaha	3555 Farnam Street Suite 1440	NE	68131	414-369-5033
Frankenmuth Mutual Ins Co	Frankenmuth	One Mutual Avenue	MI	48787	414-369-5033
Country Mutual Ins Co	Bloomington	1701 Towanda Avenue	IL	61701	414-369-5033
Cincinnati Ins Co	Fairfield	6200 South Gilmore Road	OH	45014	414-369-5033
Auto-Owners Ins Co	Lansing	6101 Anacapri Boulevard	MI	48917	414-369-5033
American Standard Ins Co of WI	Madison	6000 American Parkway	WI	53783	414-369-5033
Acuity A Mutual Ins Co	Sheboygan	2800 South Taylor Drive	WI	53081	414-369-5033

Wyoming

A-

Name	City	Address	State	Zip	Telephone
Cincinnati Indemnity Co	Fairfield	6200 South Gilmore Road	OH	45014	414-369-5033

B+

Name	City	Address	State	Zip	Telephone
USAA General Indemnity Co	San Antonio	9800 Fredericksburg Road	TX	78288	414-369-5033
USAA Casualty Ins Co	San Antonio	9800 Fredericksburg Road	TX	78288	414-369-5033
Travelers Indemnity Co	Hartford	One Tower Square	CT	6183	414-369-5033
Travelers Casualty & Surety Co	Hartford	One Tower Square	CT	6183	414-369-5033
State Farm Mutual Automobile Ins Co	Bloomington	One State Farm Plaza	IL	61710	414-369-5033
State Farm Fire & Cas Co	Bloomington	One State Farm Plaza	IL	61710	414-369-5033
Sentry Ins A Mutual Co	Stevens Point	1800 North Point Drive	WI	54481	414-369-5033
Sentry Casualty Co	Stevens Point	1800 North Point Drive	WI	54481	414-369-5033
Securian Casualty Co	St. Paul	400 Robert Street North	MN	55101	414-369-5033
Geico General Ins Co	Omaha	3555 Farnam Street Suite 1440	NE	68131	414-369-5033
Frankenmuth Mutual Ins Co	Frankenmuth	One Mutual Avenue	MI	48787	414-369-5033
Cincinnati Ins Co	Fairfield	6200 South Gilmore Road	OH	45014	414-369-5033
Acuity A Mutual Ins Co	Sheboygan	2800 South Taylor Drive	WI	53081	414-369-5033

Appendix

Quote Comparison Worksheet

Using the worksheet below is a great way to stay organized as you compare the premium quotes from different insurance companies. It allows you to easily compare companies and how much they will charge you for each type of coverage you may be considering.

If you are planning to contact more than three companies, be sure to make copies of this worksheet beforehand.

Company Name						
Phone # or Web Address						
	Limit/Deductible	Price	Limit/Deductible	Price	Limit/Deductible	Price
Bodily Injury						
Property Damage						
Medical Payments /Personal Injury Payments						
Un/Under Insured Motorist						
Collision						
Comprehensive						
Roadside Assistance						
Rental Car Reimbursement						
Loan/Lease Payoff						
Other						
Discounts						
TOTAL						

Helpful Resources

Contact any of the following organizations for further information about purchasing auto insurance.

Your state department of insurance – See next page for a specific contact

National Association of Insurance Commissioners – www.naic.org

Insurance Information Institute – www.iii.org

Independent Insurance Agents & Brokers of America – www.independentagent.com/default.aspx

Weiss Ratings, LLC. – www.weissratings.com

The following is a partial listing of websites that give auto insurance quotes

Weiss Ratings does not endorse any of these companies, nor do we warranty any of the information you may obtain from these sites. This information is being provided strictly for your reference only to show the vast number of sites available when shopping for auto insurance.

Company websites

www.21st.com	www.LibertyMutual.com
https://aarp.thehartford.com	www.nationalgeneral.com
www.Allstate.com	www.Nationwide.com
www.ElectricInsurance.com	www.Progressive.com
www.Esurance.com	www.StateAuto.com
www.Geico.com	www.StateFarm.com
www.USAA.com	

Independent websites

www.AutoInsuranceGroup.com	https://squeeze.com
www.Insurance.com	www.trustedchoice.com
www.Insure.com	

State Insurance Commissioners'
Departmental Contact Information

State	*Official's Title*	*Website Address*	*Phone Number*
Alabama	Commissioner	www.aldoi.gov	(334) 269-3550
Alaska	Director	https://www.commerce.alaska.gov/web/ins/	(907) 269-7900
Arizona	Director	https://insurance.az.gov/	(602) 364-3100
Arkansas	Commissioner	www.insurance.arkansas.gov	(501) 371-2600
California	Commissioner	www.insurance.ca.gov	(916) 492-3500
Colorado	Commissioner	https://dora.colorado.gov/	(303) 894-7499
Connecticut	Commissioner	https://portal.ct.gov/cid	(860) 297-3800
Delaware	Commissioner	https://insurance.delaware.gov/	(302) 674-7300
Dist. of Columbia	Commissioner	http://disb.dc.gov/	(202) 727-8000
Florida	Commissioner	www.floir.com/	(850) 413-3140
Georgia	Commissioner	www.oci.ga.gov/	(404) 656-2070
Hawaii	Commissioner	http://cca.hawaii.gov/ins/	(808) 586-2790
Idaho	Director	www.doi.idaho.gov	(208) 334-4250
Illinois	Director	/www2.illinois.gov/	(217) 558-2757
Indiana	Commissioner	www.in.gov/idoi/	(317) 232-2385
Iowa	Commissioner	https://iid.iowa.gov/	(515) 654-6600
Kansas	Commissioner	https://insurance.kansas.gov/	(785) 296-3071
Kentucky	Commissioner	https://insurance.ky.gov/ppc/new_default.aspx	(502) 564-3630
Louisiana	Commissioner	www.ldi.la.gov/	(225) 342-5900
Maine	Superintendent	www.maine.gov/pfr/insurance/	(207) 624-8475
Maryland	Commissioner	http://insurance.maryland.gov/Pages/default.aspx	(410) 468-2000
Massachusetts	Commissioner	https://www.mass.gov/orgs/division-of-insurance	(617) 521-7794
Michigan	Director	http://www.michigan.gov/difs	(517) 284-8800
Minnesota	Commissioner	http://mn.gov/commerce/	(651) 539-1500
Mississippi	Commissioner	http://www.mid.ms.gov/	(601) 359-3569
Missouri	Director	www.insurance.mo.gov	(573) 751-4126
Montana	Commissioner	http://csimt.gov/	(406) 444-2040
Nebraska	Director	www.doi.nebraska.gov/	(402) 471-2201
Nevada	Commissioner	www.doi.nebraska.gov/	(775) 687-0700
New Hampshire	Commissioner	www.nh.gov/insurance/	(603) 271-2261
New Jersey	Commissioner	www.state.nj.us/dobi/	(609) 292-7272
New Mexico	Superintendent	www.osi.state.nm.us/	(505) 827-4601
New York	Superintendent	www.dfs.ny.gov/	(212) 709-3500
North Carolina	Commissioner	https://www.ncdoi.gov/	(919) 807-6000
North Dakota	Commissioner	https://www.insurance.nd.gov/	(701) 328-2440
Ohio	Director	www.insurance.ohio.gov	(614) 644-2658
Oklahoma	Commissioner	https://www.oid.ok.gov/	(405) 521-2828
Oregon	Insurance Commissioner	http://dfr.oregon.gov/Pages/index.aspx	(503) 947-7980
Pennsylvania	Commissioner	www.insurance.pa.gov/	(717) 787-7000
Puerto Rico	Commissioner	https://ocs.pr.gov/English/Pages/default.aspx	(787) 304-8686
Rhode Island	Superintendent	https://dbr.ri.gov/contact/	(401) 462-9500
South Carolina	Director	www.doi.sc.gov	(803) 737-6160
South Dakota	Director	http://dlr.sd.gov/insurance/default.aspx	(605) 773-3563
Tennessee	Commissioner	http://tn.gov/commerce/	(615) 741-2241
Texas	Commissioner	www.tdi.texas.gov/	(512) 676-6000
Utah	Commissioner	www.insurance.utah.gov	(801) 957-9200
Vermont	Commissioner	www.dfr.vermont.gov/	(802) 828-3301
Virgin Islands	Lieutenant Governor	https://ltg.gov.vi/	(340) 774-7166
Virginia	Commissioner	https://scc.virginia.gov/pages/Home	(804) 371-9741
Washington	Commissioner	www.insurance.wa.gov	(360) 725-7000
West Virginia	Commissioner	www.wvinsurance.gov	(304) 558-3354
Wisconsin	Commissioner	https://oci.wi.gov/Pages/Homepage.aspx	(608) 266-3586
Wyoming	Commissioner	http://doi.wyo.gov/	(307) 777-7401

What Our Ratings Mean

A   **Excellent.** The company offers excellent financial security. It has maintained a conservative stance in its investment strategies, business operations and underwriting commitments. While the financial position of any company is subject to change, we believe that this company has the resources necessary to deal with severe economic conditions.

B   **Good.** The company offers good financial security and has the resources to deal with a variety of adverse economic conditions. It comfortably exceeds the minimum levels for all of our rating criteria, and is likely to remain healthy for the near future. However, in the event of a severe recession or major financial crisis, we feel that this assessment should be reviewed to make sure that the firm is still maintaining adequate financial strength.

C   **Fair.** The company offers fair financial security and is currently stable. But during an economic downturn or other financial pressures, we feel it may encounter difficulties in maintaining its financial stability.

D   **Weak.** The company currently demonstrates what, in our opinion, we consider to be significant weaknesses which could negatively impact policyholders. In an unfavorable economic environment, these weaknesses could be magnified.

E   **Very Weak.** The company currently demonstrates what we consider to be significant weaknesses and has also failed some of the basic tests that we use to identify fiscal stability. Therefore, even in a favorable economic environment, it is our opinion that policyholders could incur significant risks.

F   **Failed.** The company is deemed failed if it is either 1) under supervision of an insurance regulatory authority; 2) in the process of rehabilitation; 3) in the process of liquidation; or 4) voluntarily dissolved after disciplinary or other regulatory action by an insurance regulatory authority.

+   The **plus sign** is an indication that the company is in the upper third of the letter grade.

–   The **minus sign** is an indication that the company is in the lower third of the letter grade.

U   **Unrated.** The company is unrated for one or more of the following reasons: (1) total assets are less than $1 million; (2) premium income for the current year was less than $100,000; or (3) the company functions almost exclusively as a holding company rather than as an underwriter; or, (4) in our opinion, we do not have enough information to reliably issue a rating.

Glossary

This glossary contains the most important terms used in this publication.

Agent	An insurance professional that sells insurance for one or more insurance companies. Exclusive agents sell for one company while independent agents sell for more than one company.
Assigned risk plan	A state supervised program that assigns a person to a company for insurance because that person cannot get auto insurance from a regular carrier.
Book value	The value of your vehicle as determined by your insurance company.
Claim	A request to your insurance company to pay for your loss or damage you caused that is covered under your insurance policy. First-party claims are your claims to your company, and third-party claims are your claims against another person's insurance company.
Collision coverage	Optional insurance that pays for damage to your car caused by a collision with another car or object.
Comprehensive coverage	Optional insurance which pays for damage to your vehicle caused by items other than collision such as vandalism, theft, fire, or hail among other items.
Deductible	A type of loss that your policy will not cover.
Exclusion	A type of loss that your policy will not cover.
First-party claims	Your claims made to your own insurance company as opposed to third-party claims that you make to another person's insurance company.
Gap coverage	An extra coverage that can be purchased to cover the difference between the amount you owe on your vehicle and the amount the insurance company will pay you. This coverage is usually for leased vehicles but can also be purchased for vehicles that are financed.

Insurance department	A state agency that monitors insurance company activities in that state. It also assists consumers with insurance issues such as complaints and education.
Liability	A legally enforceable financial obligation.
Liability coverage	Insurance which pays for the losses of other people which you cause accidentally or negligently. Bodily injury liability pays for medical costs of others and your legal costs if a suit is brought. Property damage liability pays for damage you cause to some else's car or property.
Medical payments coverage	Optional insurance in states without "no-fault" insurance. This coverage pays for medical expenses and funeral expenses for you and your passengers regardless of who is at fault.
Negligence	Failure to exercise a generally acceptable level of care and caution.
No-fault insurance	Insurance under which each driver seeks payment from his or her own insurance company regardless of fault.
Personal Injury Protection (PIP)	A broader form of medical payments insurance coverage that offers protection for expenses incurred up to a specific, per-person dollar amount. Mandatory coverage in states with no-fault statutes, and optional in states without no-fault coverage.
Policy period	The length of time an insurance policy is valid.
Premium	The amount of money you pay for coverage.
Subrogation	The act of an insurance company seeking reimbursement from another insurance company for an amount they paid to their own policyholder for an accident in which the other company's policyholder was at fault.
Under- or uninsured motorist coverage	Insurance which pays for accidents caused by someone who has insufficient coverage or no coverage at all. This includes hit-and-run drivers.